Mantras for Managers

THE DIALOGUES WITH YETI

Mantras for Managers

THE DIALOGUES WITH YETI

N K SINGH

PENTAGON PRESS
NEW DELHI

Sixth Edition: New Delhi, 2004
Fifth Edition: New Delhi, 2001
First Edition: New Delhi, 1990

ISBN 81-86830-98-7

Published by
PENTAGON PRESS
101, AVG Bhawan, M-3, Connaught Circus,
New Delhi-110001 (India)
Phones: 011-23415198, 23415205 • Fax: 011-51517091
e-mail: rajanarya@vsnl.com

Printed by
ELEGANT PRINTERS
New Delhi-110064

To
The Spirit of Yeti
Free, Natural, Primordial
and Loving

Contents

Introduction

In 1983, I was conducting the first Asian Workshop on Human Resource Development (HRD) for airlines at Kathmandu, when I had a tryst with Yeti. After the first article, which appeared in *Abhigyan*, the journal which I edited in the Autumn of 1983, I received very encouraging letters from many eminent professionals. I decided to continue the Dialogue and the final chapter was written in the Autumn of 1988-exactly five years after the tryst. During these five years, I continued my journey of exploration and discovery through ecstasy and turmoil in a very rough terrain with all its ups and downs. The Dialogues too got mixed up with my personal experiences and insights. Some people still ask me: "Have you really seen Yeti?" My answer is: "Have you really seen yourself?" One can perhaps see oneself only in the mirror. I learnt recently when the doctor prescribed spectacles that what I saw of myself was totally different from what I thought of myself everyday for the last many years. Moreover, I am always sceptical about mirrors and cameras for their power, accuracy and realism. Besides all this, sunshine, or the absence of it, played havoc with my own images. Which one was myself? Or, all that was there did it really mirror me? Nevertheless, Yeti became a reality as much as the fictitious lion, whose stories I told my younger son Meetu, was a reality for him when he actually noticed a lion's footprints in the mud next morning. I had no business to condemn his experience as illusion since I too had only illusions.

Sometimes I see and don't see — say, when I am absorbed in my thoughts. Sometimes I don't see but still I see—as in dreams. But both are real in one form that matters to me. For example, when I cause an accident without seeing, or get excited with a dream for years. What makes a difference to all states is the experience of reality. Yeti, as such, is an experience. In this book, we have dealt with experiencing and experience.

The modern-day world would be dead without organisations. They give it an order, comfort, and resources for development. Within these 'bubbles' we live a life. How we look at these bubbles makes them what they are, since we constantly re-shape them, change them to meet stated tasks or goals. Goals become psycho-maps, which we tread, sometimes blindly, sometimes consciously. Happiness and achievement are the outcomes of our having built transactable maps and fulfillment. Stress and depression result from their all engulfing oppression. Even family is an organisation, which creates its own bubble. We live in multiple bubbles, carrying our ecstasy and agony from one to the other. But the core of all this transition lies in the man himself. 'The Dialogues', therefore, is an inquiry into man and his bubbles. It follows the experiential way to understand these. There are flashes, blind alleys and hind-sights. You may go through these not as a text-book or a novel but as you travel through a mountain range — up and down—looking at lakes, snows, trees and deep unfathomable crags and crevices. Look out for avalanches and glaciers. On the way Nachiketa is a good companion. He talks and talks. Basically, he represents a sense of wonder but his persistent endeavour to know, feel and dream is the stuff which dialogues are made of. The story of the *Katha-Upanisad* starts with Nachiketa being sent to Death, when he questions his father's hollow charity by the persistent question "Dear father, to whom will thou give me?" Nachiketa becomes a similarly persistent questioner for the Death god 'Yama' when his angry father, a King, gives him to Yama.

"This doubt that arises, consequent on the death of a man —some saying. 'It exists', and others saying. It does not exist—I would know this, under your instruction. Of all the boons, this one is the third boon."

"If you think some other boon to be equal to this, ask for that. As for wealth and long life. O Nachiketa, you become a ruler over a vast region. I make you fit for the enjoyment of all delectable things."

"O Death, tell us of that thing about which people entertain doubt in the context of the next world and whose knowledge leads to a great result. Apart from the boon, which relates to the inscrutable thing, Nachiketa does not pray for any other."

After having rejected the offer of all materialistic pleasures of the world, Nachiketa persists on knowing the essence of existence and true knowledge.

Nachiketa and Yeti have represented to me two sides of the psyche: one that is rational, systematic, analytic and high-tech. The other subterranean, primordial, original and imaginative. Incidentally, it seems to conform to two parts of the brain. Both are true and both are untrue. The synthesist school, which was advocated in the book 'Corporate Soul', is really the answer for organisations of tomorrow. The synthesists do not merely have a holistic outlook—which means looking at totality, but are much more than this. They can be said to represent a new holographic world picture, which is based on harmony of many dissimilar elements. Already a new paradigm is emerging in several sciences looking for "the pattern of relatedness" in the micro-constituents with the macrocosm. Synthesists seek the Ariadne's thread to bind apparently non-conforming realities. The psycho-unity—or the faith that spirit is one throughout all living and non-living beings, provides the glue to the synthesists. It would be observed that in Nachiketa and Yeti's interaction, they start introjecting each other. They start learning each other's language and ways of living. Moreover, yak, mountains, aeroplanes and drinks are involved in the same psycho-unity frame.

Some readers asked me why I should preach drinking via Yeti's gulps and promote Scotch. I have not attached any moral significance to such acts. If we look at Hindu mythology, it is not uncommon to know Shiva dancing, making love, devastating, taking intoxicants, and even sucking poison. Life is not seen as black or white vision. A synthesist's vision is colour vision like the hues of a colour wheel. But all this results in white when the wheel is in motion. The states of mind and behaviour have to be viewed from the kaleidoscopic viewpoint. When Mahatma Gandhi ran after a goat, in the midst of an important political discussion, the behaviour looked queer to many. Mahatma never explained it but one can empathise with his child-like love and sensitivity to all forms of life. Yeti's behaviour has to be understood in terms of his natural instincts and pure vision.

Science, philosophy and art need to find common bondages. The exclusion of one from the other has created a lopsided vision of life. The pattern that connects things with one another in this macrocosm and yesterday with today and tomorrow is "this vision thing." When Indian philosophy referred to *satyam, shivam* and *sundaram* (truth, goodness and beauty), a synthesist view of a whole world, a whole man, a whole nature was sought to be created. This apex synthesist approach needs to guide like a mission all actions of people. When we discover beauty and joy in the feeling, we are close to Brahma or Hiranyagarbha. Each man can afford as today he can afford—a TV or Video—a Brahma view. It is not a religious or sectarian view but a compatible view of life—the ultimate test of which is feeling.

Let us then study these dialogues with a poetic inspiration to gain flashes of insight into organisational sphere, which this world has become. Also let us flow with the natural charm of Nachiketa and Yeti's romantic search for improving small work organisations and the life itself. Let us also constantly wonder at its mystery.

I read a lot on quality of worklife. The more I read about this the more I am perplexed. "We are searching physical and quantitative measurements against pure economic indicators. But this search, we are again running the same rat race of Galilean and Newtonian physics. As Marxism and Capitalism have become indistinguishable today due to their obsessive pursuit of a common aim, i.e., materialism, we are confusing economics and quality of life concepts with quantity. In my view, quality of mind—a state which distinguishes Nachiketa and Yeti from Duryodhana, Dushasana and Shakuni,* is more important. It is the qualitative aspect, which can *be felt, assessed, judged* but not accurately measured in the barometer or statistics. While quantitatives will remain significant, a synthesist view will look forward to a preponderant quality to enrich and enhance life.

N.K. SINGH

*Noble and vicious characters in ancient Indian Scriptures.

Acknowledgements

I am grateful to readers and eminent social scientists who have reviewed and encouraged the work. Both at home and in the global sector I have received a very delightful response. My students and the working managers who read the work have also contributed their support to my continuing efforts to present this work in its new incarnation. My publisher has steadfastly supported originality and creativity. Major Apurva Singh, my son made many useful alterations and Shivani, corrected the proofs. Deepika's contribution to the present edition is unforgettable in taking care of precise editing of the product, which is in your hands. I would be happy to hear from the readers who wish to send me their reactions and feelings.

01-01-2004

PROFESSOR N K SINGH

narinderksingh@vsnl.net
Shivalik Ashram
Suhin, Tensil Amb
Distt. Una,
Himachal Pradesh

Chapter 1

Why Development?

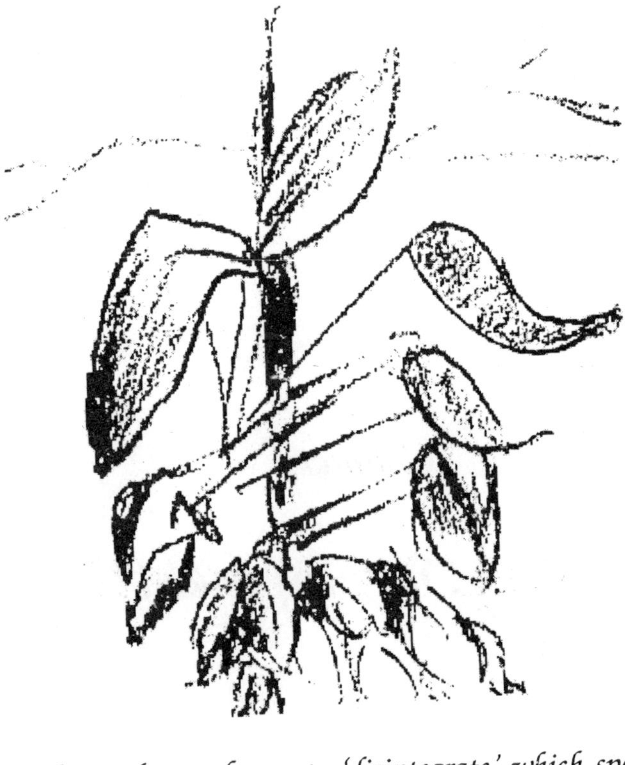

"It is the tendency of man to 'disintegrate' which spells ruin. Mankind will always bind itself with such sensitive souls who feel the pain of others, like Siddhartha did. In fact, I think it is these two forces, viz., integrative and disintegrative ones, that make the difference. People who are perceptive to the invisible ripples of interrelatedness, see the totality of the life pattern. People who divide themselves from others in their egoistic, narrow pursuits are ignored of the laws of nature."

7 Mantras for Managers

- ☆ *Cultivate learning culture.*
- ☆ *Stimulate a desire to innovate and create.*
- ☆ *Think, imagine and dream.*
- ☆ *Translate dreams into reality.*
- ☆ *Learn to explore insightful and meaningful experience. It is the truth of genuine feeling that counts in the ultimate analysis.*
- ☆ *Project the quality of life and mind to sensitise the organisations.*
- ☆ *Perceive the interrelatedness of life and universe.*

Yeti: You have many airline representatives in this workshop. What do you plan to do with them?

Nachiketa: I have no aim other than making them aware: aware of their strengths, weaknesses and limitations. They should gradually discover themselves.

Yeti: Why do you cause them this pain? Why don't you go to Pokhara? If you don't mind, I could escort them to the snowbound Himalayas. They would enjoy the new experience.

Nachiketa: The learning process is always painful, though enlightening. Have you not seen a child learning to walk? Pain suffered in this process is a part of an innate urge to grow, to be, and to become.

Yeti: Why should one grow? We are all happy as we are. Look at me: I detest civilisation I like to live alone and have a good time. You must think I am a barbarian. I do not care. I lead my own enchanted life in the Himalayas, in my own world. It is self-inflicted pain to start thinking you must do something more than what you are already doing.

Nachiketa: I agree with you that it is a question of one's own values. You are happy in what you are. You may not fly in an aeroplane, work on a computer or teach in a class. You exist. And you call it life. But once you start exploring, you also start to grow more and more inquisitive about your environment. Once you develop an urge to stand, you also want to walk and run a race. You do not feel that it is enough to sleep. Partly, it is the process of life itself that forces these issues on you. Partly, it is man's desire to excel, to innovate and create that makes him bear the pain of growth.

Yeti: All the difference is caused by the intellect, and hence, all the pain. Even if you fly, train pilots in a 3-phase simulator, spend billions of dollars on new technology, you still live a life and die. The unalterable facts of birth and death are the only significant ones. How does it matter what you do between these two points of a beginning and an end? Why should people fly? Why can't they remain where they are, like me?

Nachiketa: You are very right in saying that the difference is caused by the intellect. We think, we imagine and we dream.

We get stimulated by our own images and try to translate them into reality. This is why we are caught in the vortex of a struggle for creating new civilisations.

Yeti: So what? If you do not do, what will happen? Who knows when you will meet dystopia? Who knows when all this will go up in smoke? Whither then, your workshops, machines and technology?

Nachiketa: I agree; I do not know. But as long as I live, I compete with others. I perceive other to be affluent, more comfortable, more happy and I run a race.

Yeti: You are running a meaningless race. In the end we are all the same. Your assumption that others are more happy is a mere chimera.

Nachiketa: True, but the race also matters. It is a question of aesthetics. You feel it is beautiful. There is a thrill in it. Why are you so enchanted by the snow of the Himalayas? Why can't you admire the dusty gusts of a desert? Is it simply because you were born in the folds of a mountain, and not in sand dunes.

Yeti: Perhaps, yes. But I like my hills.

Nachiketa: Herein lie the fundamentals of our views. The difference is a difference of accident. We love what we find harmonious with our style of existence, or, perhaps, what we become accustomed to. Why can't you travel to metropolitan cities, feel the pulse of the jet-set era, and enjoy other materialistic pleasures. I am sure if you swill Scotch whisky for a year, you will start loving it. You basically like what you are used to. So do we love what we have. We also love to have more of what others have.

Yeti: True, but the problem lies in your hankering after 'more'. The words 'growth' and 'development' are synonymous with having more and more of what you have. This process is painful. Even discovering oneself is painful. So why do it? If ultimately we care for beauty and feeling, why do all this? You can find immense joy in what you have.

Nachiketa: This is precisely the question with which I started. It is a matter of attitudes and values. Our differences are those of thinking and imagining. But, as I said earlier, if you try it, you will be thrilled by the process. It is the process which makes life different. The end is the same for all of us.

(This conversation was disrupted on account of an urgent overseas call....)

Yeti: I am sorry that I had to leave abruptly yesterday, due to the telephone call. I thought you would be busy.

Nachiketa: Not at all. The night was as free as the chilly winds of the Himalayas. None to converse and be with. I would have liked to have continued the dialogue. In fact, I waited for you will the early hours of dawn. I waited for your wistful eyes.

Yeti: I attended the workshop. Now I am more knowledgeable and in a better position to converse about it.

Nachiketa: How did you do it? We did not see you. Did you convert yourself into a fly?

Yeti: If a thousand years ago there could be a Pushpak Viman without a pilot, and Sanjay to videotape the Mahabharata, I could also use extrasensory perception to be with you. Are you not with one whom you intensely desire or feel for? I did the same.

Nachiketa: I sometimes wonder if the hi-fi technology of today is really the latest, or whether the ancient methods were really far ahead of us.

Yeti: You know that physics is turning towards spiritualism by recognising the possibility a soul-filled universe. What was, is now, and will always be. The differences are really only differences of perception.

Nachiketa: Today you are really profound. Yesterday you questioned our process of development and the rate of technological progress, and today you seem to be the super-high technologist of our age.

Yeti: The difference lies in my understanding. Today I observed you all, and now I can communicate better. My knowledge is the same, only my words are more intelligible, and my vocabulary borrowed from your experts.

Nachiketa: I am glad. Perhaps we shall learn more from each other. But tell me, are you convinced of my thesis of value systems? Are you satisfied with my explanations?

Yeti: Not fully. Try to first answer my questions, then I shall proceed further. First, let me know how it is that you have divided the world into two hemispheres, i.e., East and West? Why are you so enamoured of the West? Why is the West not enamoured of the East?

Nachiketa: Obviously we are learning the secret of

technology. We are progressing. We want to be rich, affluent and happy.

Yeti: How do you know they are more happy?

Nachiketa: Because they are rich, they are secure.

Yeti: They have more means at their disposal, but only to lead mundane lives. Also, happiness is illusory. Security is a relative term. If you crave for happiness, why don't you arrange entertainment and sight-seeing, instead of mere 'talk, talk, talk' in your workshop. Poor David Bowers travelled thousands of miles to talk to you even when he was tired; the researchers ran helter-skelter to collect data, which was only partially revealing, about themselves. This can hardly be regarded as happiness by anyone.

Nachiketa; But this is exploration, and as I told you yesterday, it is insightful and enlightening. It is just like your wistful wandering in the Himalayas. You cannot just lie dozing in your cave.

Yeti: Okay. But do you know you have more robots in Japan than in the US? Why don't you hire them to do this for you?

Nachiketa: Because the robot is an instrument, a means, a slave. The robot does not have any intelligence or power of thought.

Yeti: What makes the difference? Memory? They have enough of it. All operations of normally programmed robots point towards enough sense, and a common artificial intelligence.

Nachiketa: True, but perhaps they lack a mind, a soul.

Yeti: Do you know that there is enough research evidence to prove that even plants and weeds, feels, discern and recognise? They have life. So who knows if robots, too, perhaps have some kind of temporary life!

Nachiketa: Even if they have, it is the quality of life we are concerned with. That is what makes the difference.

Yeti: Good. Not affluence or economic prosperity. This is precisely the point I was trying to bring home to you. The quality of life is not dependent on material possessions, but rather, the richness of ones values and thoughts. It is the truth of feeling that counts in the ultimate analysis.

Nachiketa: Yes, now I think we agree. This is the same point I have been making to you.

Yeti: My effort today is to acquaint you with the Upanishadic teachings, which thousands of years back, advocated that one must discover unity in diversity. Even if mankind is splintered into a billion parts, we much recognise the invisible links that bind them together. Intelligence really consists in becoming aware of this.

Nachiketa: I agree with you entirely. We have found the common links. We, in Asia, know that we have certain cultural specifics. There are airlines with organised labour and there are airlines without that. There are large organisations and there are small ones. There are islands of high technology and there are relatively backward ones. But men shall endure all these differences. Man Bahadur Kharakas will symbolise hope and concern for people. They will bring a sensitive culture to organisations; they will lend differentia to an airline, a country, a nation, a world. It is the tendency of man to 'disintegrate', which spells ruin. Mankind will always bind itself with such sensitive souls who feel the pain of others, like Siddhartha did. In fact, I think it is these two forces, viz., integrative and disintegrative ones, that make the difference. People who are perceptive to the invisible ripples of interrelatedness, see the totality of the life pattern. People who divide themselves from others in their egoistic, narrow pursuits, are ignorant of the laws of nature.

Yeti: Very true. It is neither my being alone, nor your being in a group which is of importance. What matters is a cognizance of the basic unity of mankind in spite of all this diversity. Having grasped this, we have to build our values on this foundation. Let not technology and materialism erect impermeable barriers between men. Let the spirit of common enquiry into our true natures and of the interrelatedness of existence rise to the fore, helping us to create a society both sensitive and human. Let the robots, planes and computers not blur the vision of the mind, of the soul—which are perennial, binding threads. Let temporary dazzling illusions not blind us to the commonness of our destinies.

Nachiketa: I think we see a lot of sense in it. Let us pray that in future we are saved from ad hoc politicisation, single-minded technology and irrationalism. Man must find solace in discovering the truth of unity in diversity, a pattern of interrelatedness, and a universe which is based on conception of beauty to be felt and experienced, not computerised and stored.

(At this moment he heard the giggles of someone. Yeti looked tense. He left without a word. No one yet knows if he was disturbed by the laughter or whether he went after it).

Chapter 2

Why Organisations?

The group, or an organisation, also depends largely on its members, for a unique characteristic emerges from collective interaction, which is not merely a summation of individual abilities, but more than that—both special as well as superior. This depends on the way an organisation arranges its tasks, roles and system, as also the manner in which the ideology of an organisation influences its people. Sometimes organisations do become cages. Individuals are deprived of their freedom by the very process of uniformity and standardisation. New constraints emerge, which enslave initiative and creation. Mediocrity and averageness become the passwords.

7 Mantras for Managers

- ☆ *Introduce co-ordination, communication and competition to provide a climate for excellence.*
- ☆ *Understand the inherent purposes of the organisation and mould the organisation according to these purposes.*
- ☆ *Learn to outgrow mental colour blindness when only black and white vision exist. Such men do not understand the splendours spectrum of the colour wheel.*
- ☆ *Observe varying options and differentiation of organisational life.*
- ☆ *Ensure the entry of competent and committed persons in an organisation to make it effective.*
- ☆ *Provide ample freedom to develop creativity and quality of life in the organisation.*
- ☆ *Avoid distortions in organisations resulting from personality defects in leaders, distortions in communication, long chain of bureaucracy and excessive secretiveness or indifference to individuals' aspirations for growth.*

Yeti: I think our dialogue is now taking shape. I am learning more and more about your organisations, the human webs which you have created for keeping everyone busy.

Nachiketa: I am glad you are back. Where did you disappear last night?

Yeti: Well, don't ask me about that. I don't think I know myself. Let us continue our conversation.

Nachiketa: Today you raise a new point. You are now questioning our organisations. You must not forget that the phenomenal development which marks the history of man is all due to organisations. An organisation makes a man greater than what he actually is, and capable of doing enormous and complicated tasks. An organisation imparts efficiency to society.

Yeti: Let us not raise the question of progress and development. We have noticed that it might be an illusion, or at best, a viewpoint. You say it is the process which you find beautiful: No arguments can dismantle that premise. But nevertheless, the issue of human monoliths remains to be debated.

Nachiketa: An organisation, my dear friend, is more than a man. It is greater than a man because it uses the intellect, perception, vision and sensibilities of many men all at once. If you concede that one plus one is two, then you cannot but agree that an organisation must result in *summun bonum*.

Yeti: Numerically, ten is more than one. But qualitatively, one may be greater than one hundred. Can you say that one hundred rats are better than a man?

Nachiketa: I do see your point. It is not *ipso facto* true that an organisation represents a qualitatively superior configuration than a single man. It all depends on who constitute that organisation. But, if you have people of high calibre, you are bound to have an organisation with almost superhuman capabilities.

Yeti: I am glad you recognised my input. But, let us now imagine a situation where you have a multiplicity of men of high calibre in an organisation. You may come face to face with dysfunctional relationships and a dismal output. Firstly, they may not see eye to eye, and if this is so, you might well have an organisation, but also a disjointed collection of unconcerned people. This will be harmful to all, rather than bringing about your concept of *summum bonum*. Secondly, there may be a *persona non grata*, because he is the oddman-out. This can harm him as well as the organisation. Thirdly, a collection of men has many restraining influences. Men, out of sheer deference, fear, inability to communicate with people the consider inferior, or even out of sheer conformism, perpetuate *status quo*, or mediocrity. In other words, the survival instinct of the organisation itself may be a burden on the quality and effectiveness of performance.

Nachiketa: I agree that these are the possible blind spots of an organisation. But the remains, that given the necessary co-ordination, communication and competition, men would like to excel. The strength of an organisation lies in creating a motivated group for achieving excellence. This quest is certainly more thrilling and more fruitful than lonely wandering in the Himalayas.

Yeti: Don't be satirical. I do not think that loneliness is a qualitatively poorer experience than being in a group. But I accept that a motivated group of high calibre men will create synergy to exceed one man's output. The basic rule, therefore, would be to ensure entry of only such personnel in an organisation, who not only fit in with its search and survival charter but also find themselves at home in its culture. Above all, they are the most competent men.

Nachiketa: The group, or an organisation, also depends largely on its members, for a unique characteristic emerges from collective interaction, which is not merely a summation of individual abilities, but more than that-both special as well as superior. This depends on the way an organisation arranges its tasks, roles and systems, as also the manner in which the ideology of an organisation influences its people. Let us, therefore, sum up our thoughts.

- An effective organisation works towards ensuring maximum care in the selection of its team.
- It charges the group with the responsibility to achieve worthwhile goals. It imbues men with a mission, which acts charismatically to stir them not only to obtain the best for the organisation, but also to sacrifice self-interest in favour of organisational interest.
- It leaves them free to give more and more of themselves by looking after their needs and providing them with the necessary instruments for achieving greater success It provides them with resources which an individual would not easily obtain by himself.

Yeti: All this seems very interesting, but which type of organisation are you talking of? Is this true of all?

Nachiketa: I think it is advisable to understand the various types of organisations. Conventionally, organisations may be thought of in terms of their structural or compositional framework. We talk of corporations, government agencies, cooperatives and so on. This is only one way of looking at them, i.e., as to how they are organised, who owns them, etc. There are, however, types based on the exercise of power, e.g., moral, participative, alienative, exploitative, etc. I do not consider such a classification very meaningful, since you can change the way power is exercised, whereas it is the ends which really determine how an organisation comes into being. I prefer to think of organisations in terms of the goals they try to achieve. I would, therefore, classify them as under:

Goal based types	Example
Altruistic organisations Those which operate for The well-being of others.	The army, scientific institutions, Governmental organisations, social welfare groups, Political parties, social institutions, educational bodies.
Group interest organisations Those which have the group's/ member's/owner's interests as their primary aim.	Private companies, unions, associations, cooperatives, clubs, religious groups etc.
Self interest organisations Those which operate entirely for the organiser's for own interest.	Small shops, trading bodies, farming etc.

In the above typology the extent of social ideology gradually diminishes as one moves from top to bottom. The individual's self-interest increases in the same order. In my view, this is a crucial issue, making for significant differences from one type to another. The goals, therefore, constitute the *raison d'etre* of an organisation, and provide the basis for a durable classification. Here, I may mention that all classifications are meant only as aids for understanding. In reality, there are no watertight divisions. Society is made up of multipurpose and pluralistic sub-systems.

Yeti: Ha! Ha! Ha! How artificially complicated a life you lead. I have only the high and low peaks of the mountains to contend with, and a reasonably happy life without organisations.

Nachiketa: I see your point. But remember, maturity and growth mean differentiation. That is where the richness of life lies. An infant has a simple life space. He can only differentiate between himself and the life giving nipple. It is only later, that he discovers the endless variety of life. An intelligent and accomplished man has a far more differentiated life space. Syllogism for the Greeks had three premises, and for the logic of Indians five. There might be more. It depends on our ability to see life. A man afflicted with colour blindness sees only black, white and grey. He misses out on the splendid spectrum of the colour wheel. Both may be happy, but one has a richer store of experience.

Yeti: But why should one see all this?

Nachiketa: Let us not go back to issues that we have already resolved.

Yeti: Okay! Let us continue with your organisationology. (Nachiketa offers a drink to Yeti, who gulps it down)

Nachiketa: Let us now revert to our topic. As you know, the organisation is an instrument for achieving co-ordination of various resources, including human; it represents a team effort for achieving goals which contribute to development.

Yeti: But there can be organisations of law-breakers too. Why have you not spoken of those?

Nachiketa: I agree that even anti-social elements may use this instrument to augment their power and use resources for their own ends. They, too, get organised and difficult to handle. The basic problems of all organisations are similar, the difference lies only in the goals. Here we are speaking of organisations which do not fall within the three categories mentioned by me, but represent a fourth one, which we can call "anti-social organisations." These would include gangs of bootleggers, immoral traffickers, thieves, robbers and dacoits, etc. The problems of their functioning are the same.

Yeti: How can you compare the processes of such illegal institutions with those of altruistic ones? It seems absurd.

Nachiketa: Yes, but look at the following characteristics of an organisation:

- An organisation is a collection of more than one man working for common objectives in a co-ordinated manner.
- It ensures communication amongst its members and with outsiders.
- It rewards, punishes, encourages and responds to people.
- It collects information from the environment, which it processes for its own use.
- It copes with changes within its fold and those which take place in the environment.
- It uses technology, skill, knowhow, to get work done.
- It has a personality. It draws, expends energy, has unique characteristics, and some conscious and unconscious areas.

Basically, therefore, it is a network for communicating, exercising power, using technology or skills and co-ordinating the activities of people. These are common to all organisations; only the ends differ, and lend a distinct character to ones work. The goals become ingredients of the mission in a wider sense.

Yeti: You are only speaking about the characteristics and goals of an organisation. You presume these bring about desirable changes in society. But I am more interested in knowing what happens to the man, the central point. Does all this contribute to his self-fulfillment? Do not organisations contribute towards stifling man's nature and freedom?

Nachiketa: That is the other side of the coin. You have raised very pertinent issues. Sometimes organisations do become cages. Individuals are deprived of their freedom by the very process of uniformity and standardisation. New constraints emerge, which enslave initiative and creation. Mediocrity and averageness become the passwords. Let us try to understand some I these issues before we go into the dynamics of an organisation.

There are people who seem to use up all the air in the room. They have a 'larger than life' self image, a lower level of consciousness of values, of caring for others, and of enlightenment. They suffer from a delusion of grandeur or persecution. Such manic-depressive and paranoid men sap the vitality of an organisation. The problem, therefore, lies with the human being themselves, and not with the structure of an organisation as such. There has been enough talk about structures. Are they so relevant? A pervert can turn any structure, howsoever beautiful or functionally effective, into a prison. A prison is also an organisation, but one which denies freedom to its inmates in the larger interests of society. But it is so by design and objective. When other organisations acquire the characteristics of a prison, they represent a transition a dehumanised society, since the people are then punished without having committed any crimes. It is true that every organisation does denote a curtailment of individual freedom, but this has to be limited to the extent that is essential to the functioning of an organisation.

Let us now look at the following chart:

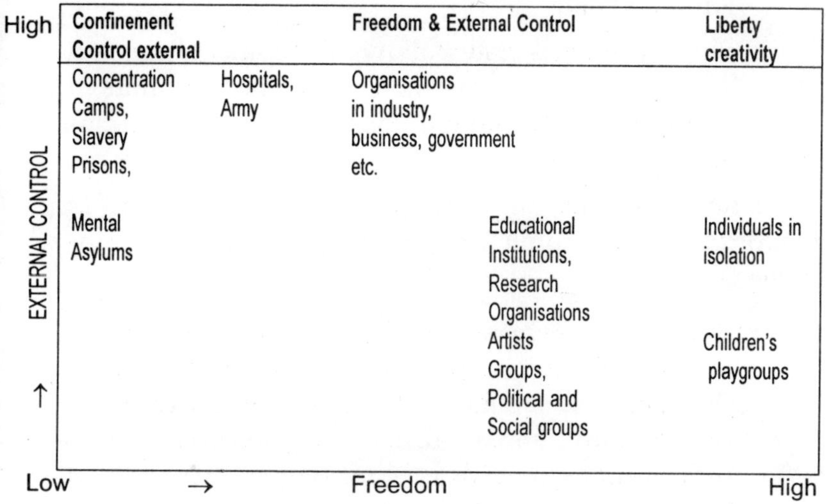

FREEDOM EXTERNAL CONTROL DIMENSION

Some of the features of the above diagram, which only shows the structural and environmental characteristics impinging on an individual's freedom are:

- Freedom is a relative concept. Complete freedom—in the absolute sense—is not possible in life, unless one achieves *Moksha* or Enlightenment.
- We have, therefore, attempted a cluster picture using as a basis the external control characteristically or typically exercised by the very nature and structure of a group.
- Freedom is essential to creativity and innovation, but freedom is not synonymous with these, nor does it produce these values by itself.
- The choice of an individual to become a member of a group entails his acceptance of the norms of

freedom prescribed in the structure. Some degree of external control is expected once an organisation admits a man.

- Beyond what is stated above, the man, culture and climate of the organisation determine the limits of freedom. In this sphere, there are wide variations and distortions.

Let us now consider the ways distortions on the norms of freedom take place in an organisation. I can tell you some of these:

- *Distortions due to personality defects of leaders*: These are reflected by the psychic disorders of the men at the helm. Some have delusions of grandeur or persecution, some suffer from excessive ego-inflation, some lack of confidence and trust in human beings who report to them and some are schizoid characters. It is very difficult to deal with such disorders unless clinical help is taken or, alternatively, changes in the leadership are effected.
- *Distortions due to communication problems*: If an organisation has clogged channels of communication, it loses its link with reality and as such, gets divorced from it. The organisation can thus lose its autonomy and rely excessively on either informal channels, or a concentration of all functions in a few people, even one man.
- *Distortions due to structure and systems*: Bureaucratic procedures, delays, excessive secretiveness, long hierarchical chains, unmanageable size and rigid structures create barriers in the way of freedom. Many creative people, therefore, find organisations too stifling.

- *Organisations not matching the individual's aspirations and growth:* In some organisations, some men grow faster than others, creating a situation where they become institutions by themselves. It is very difficult for such men to find the freedom which they need within the framework of normal organisations, unless they make special adjustments. Similarly, there are problem people, who have failed to learn and grow. They are neglected and become isolated. They are active in their own ways, with really contributing anything to the objectives of the organisation. They constitute unconscious of the organisation and need careful treatment. They find themselves" caged in.

Organisations thus become cages.

(Nachiketa looked at Yeti. Yeti was fast asleep and was emitting deep snoring sounds. The bottle of Scotch was empty. Was it the boredom of the monologue which had lulled him to sleep? Or was it the drink which had its soporific effect? Or both?)

Chapter 3

Insights on Organisations

Experiencing this unity is not possible without experience of its diversity—recognising, for instance, that in the colour wheel a gamut of hues merge into one; furthermore, that these hues are perceived as a result of colour vision, that they are not independent entities in themselves, but, rather, fragments of reality, captured through an instrument; that instruments are limited in so much as they are capable of capturing but a part of the vast sea of unlimited events, appearances and phenomena. This is akin to the process of discovering the cosmos within the self, and, the self in the cosmos.

7
Mantras for Managers

- ☆ *Clear one's receptive sensors of prejudices and dichotomy of mind between self and others.*
- ☆ *Shed narrow confines of selfishness and possessiveness.*
- ☆ *Discover interrelatedness between self and others and the universe.*
- ☆ *Experience unity in diversity.*
- ☆ *Understand both the processes of varying degrees of changes and differentiations underlying the uniqueness and unity.*
- ☆ *Synthesise Western and Eastern approaches of needs and value culture.*
- ☆ *Inculcate value guided management.*

Yeti: The concept of organisation is really quite fascinating. But, as you agreed yesterday, often the very instrument that one designs for improving performance, becomes a major impediment to human welfare.

Nachiketa: True, but these are circumstances akin to the health of the human body. When sickness prevails, we try to cure it, rather than do away with the body.

Yeti: I am sorry, but now you are hitting below the belt. I have shown you how it is possible to live happily without organisations, those large complicated artifacts. I have also followed your reasoning that growth in the materialistic and social sense presupposes effective use organisations. We have also discussed the linkage between freedom and sacrifice of freedom within the organisational framework. On the one hand, we seek liberty and, on the other, we attempt to organise our activities, only to subject ourselves to added constraints, perhaps the hope of freeing ourselves from privation and insecurity. Yet, we have seen the organisations, themselves, often become the cause of privation and insecurity. Don't you see the paradox?

Nachiketa: That is a clever observation: I note that your logic has overtaken intuitional spontaneity.

Yeti: No. I am learning to find reasons for what I happen to accept naturally and instinctively. Perhaps this argument, too, is circular.

Nachiketa: But let us also note that a healthy organisation provides for the greatest human welfare, while allowing for the achievement of work goals.

Yeti: Herein lies that fallacy of all management experts, who seek the best of both the worlds. In reality, however, it is extremely difficult to reconcile the one with the other, and it is my hypothesis that almost all organisations are characterised by a tyrannical concern for work and technology, at the expense of the goals of human development.

Nachiketa: I do see the point that production, productivity and technology should be subordinated to the end of human development and good and that ultimately, everything must be evaluated with reference to man.

Yeti: You are falling a prey to Western thought, which would lead us in a different direction. Not man, but the cosmos, is the overriding criterion—an Upanishadic concept that must remain central to our approach.

Nachiketa: Again, I must admit that you are brilliant and right. Our logic has become distorted. As human beings, we test everything from our own selfish points of view. Just as selfishness is a limiting factor for man, so is it for all mankind. We have no right to tread the path that may cause extinction of the entire universe, in order to preserve ourselves, or to advance our selfish interests. In fact, these selfish acts are only self defeating, since the entire cosmos is based on relationships of inter-dependence. Where would we be for instance without the solar system, were we to destroy it?

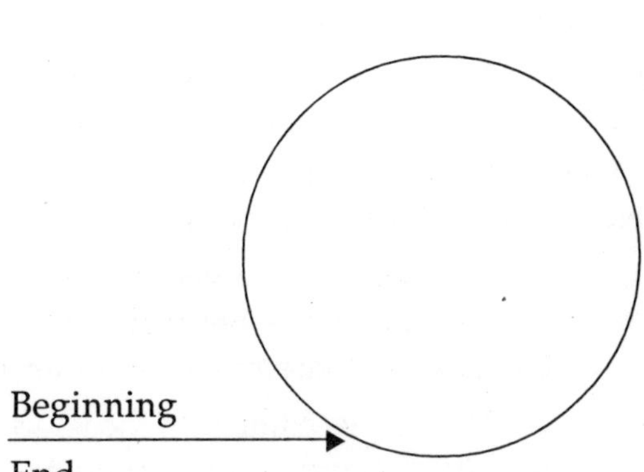

The circle below demonstrates my vision of truth. Had truth a form, it would be circular.

At some unknown point, selfishness merges into altruism and altruism into selfishness. Beginnings become ends and ends become beginnings. This perhaps explains why you found my argument circular.

Yeti: Ha! Ha!! Ha!!! Now you are practising self-deception. You cannot resolve basic organisational dilemmas by explaining the interconnections among cause and effect.

Nachiketa: We can. We must grasp the process of developing insight before we can come to understand organisations. Our tools and tackles must be cleansed if we are to evaluate others. Dirty specks only blur our vision, which explains the *Upanishad's* concern for purification of the self. This philosophical base can be summarised as under:

- Looking within to clear one's receptive sensors and judgement of prejudices is essential.
- The spiritual concept of 'I' which acts as the witness and base for all mental processes can act as the seer for this process also.
- The dichotomy of mind versus body must be transcended once we have understood the complete relationship between the two.
- Thought processes, once shorn of their selfish and possessive content, will impel one move beyond the narrow confines of the self, only to float outwards in quest of unification with cosmic processes.
- This process of reaching out, inevitably results in the discovery of a correlation between the self and others; of patterns of relatedness in the universe.
- Gradually, as differences come into focus, so does an underlying unifying bond become more discernible,

best expressed in the concept of unity in diversity and diversity in unity.

- However, experiencing this unity is not possible without experience of its diversity—recognising, for instance, that in the colour wheel a gamut of hues merge into one; furthermore, that these hues are perceived as a result of colour vision, that they are not independent entities in themselves, but, rather, fragments of reality, captured through an instrument; that instruments are limited in so much as they are capable of capturing but a part of the vast sea of unlimited events, appearances and phenomena. This is akin to the process of discovering the cosmos within the self, and the self in the cosmos.

Yeti: I do appreciate this, but how do you propose to go about operationalising all these thoughts for your "Organisationology."

Nachiketa: I shall do so, but before that, we should understand certain fundamental issues.

Yeti: How about some Scotch today? Does that unite me with Scotland?

Nachiketa: You have an uncanny habit of being facetious. (Nachiketa offers Yeti a drink, who, as usual, gulps it down neat).

Nachiketa: Yeti, now that you have started liking whisky, I think you should at least learn how to drink it.

Yeti: I only drink it if it is 'there', if it is not, I do not miss it. Yearnings do not depend on habits but needs. Some needs are cultivated, and still lead to yearnings.

Nachiketa: I think you are digressing.

Yeti: No. It is the same circular thesis. As long as one does not get bogged down by these needs, one continues to float to the ocean, like the log of wood alluded to by Buddha.

Nachiketa: Does this mean that we should opt for Sartre's "existence precedes essence" thesis?

Yeti: No, I am following Buddha's concept of flux and change. However, the change within and without does not occur in unrelated stages. For, I am a repository of several experiences, happenings and events, past and present, that have mingled and become one with me, and cannot hence, be consigned, like transitory playthings to nothingness.

Nachiketa: Let me now continue the thesis, and explain some basic methodological issues that pertain to our study of organisations.

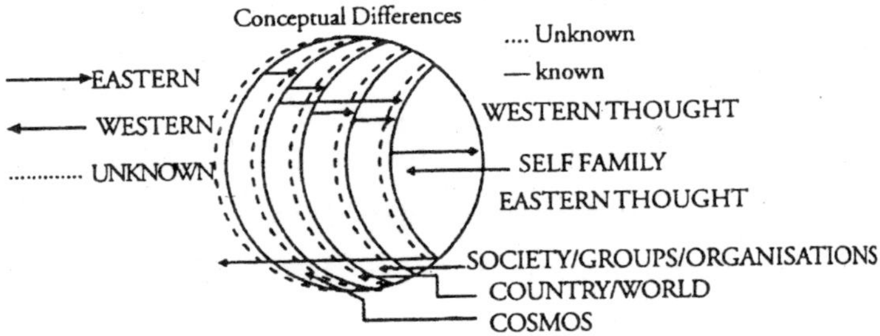

The diagram on previous page is a comparative picture of the defining features of Eastern and Western thought. These may be summarised as under:

Eastern (Indian)	Vs Accent on	Western (Greek)
• Continuities in reality	Vs	Dichoromies in reality
• Holistic relatedness and synthesis	Vs	Divisionalism and analysis
• Tentativeness	Vs	Definiteness
• Inductive reasoning	Vs	Deductive reasoning
• Intuition	Vs	Rationalism

Operationalising these differences in philosophical orientations for our study of present day organisation, we might postulate the following differences in approach:

CULTURAL DIFFERENCES IN APPROACH

Dimension	Eastern*	Western
• Individual concern	Concern for family/society	Concern for self/society
• Organisational orientation	Predominance of welfare orientation	Predominance of economic orientation
• Favourite solution to problems	Compromise, cooperation, convergence	Competition, conflict, convergence
• Outlook	Single minded purpose and concentration	Discursive and scattered direction
• Object focus	Universe	Self
• Organisational preoccupation	Misssion/ideology	Objective/targets

*This represents the Hindu, Sufi and Buddhist philosophical heritage of India, Japan, Thailand, etc., but does not completely represent the reality today in practice.

Yeti: You appear to be drawing the outline of value systems of organisations. The important question is, how do you diagnose organisation?

Nachiketa: By pinpointing the differences, I am not distinguishing systems as good or bad; I am only trying to typify some variations. Perhaps a synthesis of these different value system would provide the ideal approach. Let us now consider the operational implication of some approaches to the study of organisations; i.e., what to study and how to go about doing so.

Western Approach	Proposed Approach
• Study the structure and its effectiveness together with organisational and goals, *per se*	Study structure as a part of a total internal and external environment and organisational goals, with reference to human good.
• Study of top management	Study bottom management also
• Study high flyers	Study low performers
• Study needs	Study values
• Study leader as a performer	Study leader as a person
• Study competencies	Study total personalities
• Observation	Introspection/perception
• Rationalism and scientific analysis	Intuition and understanding
• Knowledge	Feeling

The approach that has been proposed above can be adopted to understand organisations effect improvements in them. The various methodological details involved in giving shape this approach remain to be worked out.

(Suddenly a yak rushed into the tent. In a rampage, it smashed the bottle of Scotch and crockery, tore the tent and managed to escape. Yeti ran after it. It was snowing outside, but still, one could recognise the outline of Annapurna, standing aloof and unruffled in background.)

Chapter 4

Tools for Insights: Feelings

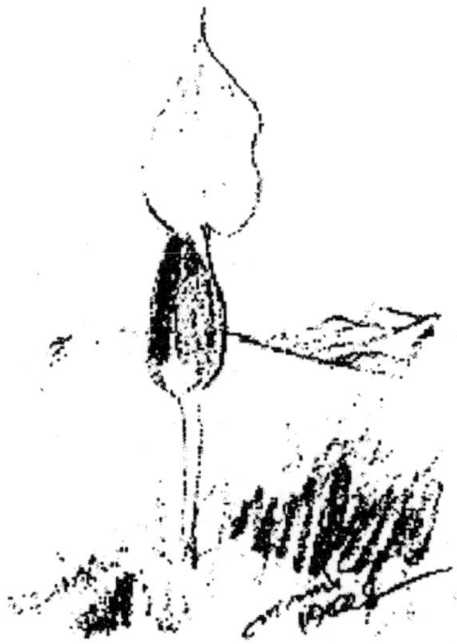

Organisational Psychounity (OPU) is a system of understanding and improving organisations. Based on research, it regards a high degree of integration as essential for effectiveness of organisations. All organisations have an essential common spirit, i.e., their mission and values. This is reflected in their shared norms and goals, called culture. The corporate culture is an indicator of the Psychounity and the Corporate Soul. OPU advocates an understanding of this unifying spirit and common perception of truth for making organisations effective. This is the school of self-realization of organisations.

7 Mantras for Managers

- *Develop feeling as a state of mind rather than body. Such feelings are not coloured by inner or outer disturbances and reflect a natural state of sensitive realization.*
- *See holistically and integrate the vision with feeling. Do not own a slice of truth. Get absorbed in it.*
- *Create patterns of interrelatedness by living through others' lives and experiences.*
- *Sharpen observation as a tool to notice expressions, colours, emotions, seasons, costumes, movements, lustre and dark corners.*
- *Shed artificiality of feeling removing suppression and hypocrisy.*
- *Learn to understand, linkage of prakriti with purusha. In other words, finding higher purpose in small actions.*
- *Identify new linkages in previously unconnected things to unleash creativity.*

Nachiketa: So here we are again after that nightmarish scene.

Yeti: Ha! Ha!! Ha!!! Let us proceed with your prescriptions for organisational insights.

Nachiketa: There are no prescriptions. We must jointly explore the realm of ideas.

Yeti: Although I don't care for search, yet let me go along with you. Personally I like to feel, which is more fundamental to a sentient being.

Nachiketa: This is exactly what I wanted to say that 'feeling' is the best methodology for understanding the organisations. But here by feeling, I do not mean mere sensation. To me, it denotes a state of mind rather than of body. It is not a search for logical relationships of things and events. It is a consciousness of consonance or dissonance, quietude or sublime state as against dullness or agitation. It is everything in oneself experiencing something.

Yeti: Are you implying then that lower animals are devoid of this feeling?

Nachiketa: I am. As you move up the evolutionary ladder you notice a certain purification of feelings. Sensation is common to all the rungs.

Yeti: Every man feels differently. How does one know whether one's feelings are right or wrong?

Nachiketa: The conception of right and wrong is an artifact of mind. Only one must ensure certain prerequisites to develop feelings so that these are not coloured by inner or outer disturbances. A natural state of feeling is not an artificially cultivated syndrome, affected style or preconceptions. There are no differences in that natural state.

Yeti: O.K., let us know how to develop this tool. Even to be natural, one has to learn.

Nachiketa: Yes. One has to. The problem lies in our getting conditioned to certain values through a distorted upbringing. A child comes into the world with natural feelings, but he gradually learns the use of make-up to alter their appearance in the course of development. In part he looks up at elders and assimilates their behaviour or values. Simultaneously, however, he is unable to grow out of his infantile non-concern with the integrated order of the cosmos. Initially he unconsciously lives it. In the first case, he learns about right and wrong, good and bad, desirable and undesirable notions. In the latter case, he simply fails to see the linkage of self and cosmos. A baby differentiates between self and the life giving nipple of a benevolent mother. As he grows, he learns to satisfy himself. His 'self comes before others. He learns to subdue the self. He does not learn to integrate it with the universal spirit of love and feeling. Or, perhaps learns it only in flashes of ecstasy, realisation, tragedy or enlightenment later. Most men continue to live like overgrown children, as they fail to learn this integration. Self realisation means recovering unconscious infantile participation in censive purpose, consciously with intense awareness. The result of this failure is conflict, greed, exploitation and deceit. They are no longer natural, their feelings are contorted and coloured, the feeling of oneness with the broader social and cosmic purpose is a natural one. We emerge, from the womb of *Prakriti* to forget our purpose of *Purusha*. The disunity and fragmentation are fatal to the naturalness. Those who become conscious of society by suppression of their selfish motives, only 'feel' but partially, since the suppression haunts the self dynamically. It throttles the naturalness. Only realisation of universal interlinkages can take away the artificiality.

Yeti: To me it appears rather silly that one should learn to love everyone.

Nachiketa: Not love, but develop feelings in a natural way—in a way that when you 'feel', you 'know'.

Yeti: Is it something like intuition?

Nachiketa: Not quite. Intuition refers to immediate knowledge without logical reasoning or evidence. But 'feeling' is experiencing and knowing together. You will understand it if I give an example. Suppose you enter an organisation that is new to you. When you look around, the faces of people, their actions, their expressions and their work, all start speaking to you and you do get a certain feeling. You might not have worked out an in-depth analysis of what is going on, but you do get a feel of the place. The more natural you are, the more accurate your feelings are likely to be. This 'feel' of an organisation is a sure indication of its state of health. You have to feel your way through in bringing release to an organisation from its sickness and put it on the road to recovery.

Yeti: This seems a highly mystic and somewhat irrational approach.

Nachiketa: You may call it what you wish but the fact remains that you cannot wish away the reality of feeling. Were you to sit in the vicinity of a criminal or saint, you would get a certain feeling about them even without knowing who they are. When you are engaged in creative work you know in a flash of feeling when your work has reached a stage of completion. Mattisse often in doing a painting used to say 'Now it looks at me' and that, for him was the stage of completion. If you want to use a computer to capture and forecast this state of feeling precisely, you cannot. It is just a pure feel-natural, unbiased, but sensitive.

To develop this:

- One has to cleanse perception. It requires learning to be able to see without favourable or unfavourable apperceptions. It is not enough to just observe, but also to penetrate minor changes in sensory data, e.g., facial expressions, colour, moods, seasons, postures, movements, polish, luster and dark corners.
- One has to see that whole, not only parts. People tend to see what they want to see, and in wanting to see, are limited by self-interest. Transcending selfishness to link oneself with others, you can also see what others see. You see the pattern of a gestalt and not the private world of your own ambitions and fears. This kind of seeing is also feeling your way into interconnections. One knows more than a narrow, individual version of truth, which is hardly enough. Organisational Psychounity says "do not own a slice of truth, get absorbed in it." You become part of a large self. It does not mean you lose your identity. It only means exchanging the solidity of selfish *tininess* with extended life in others, through whom you taste the multifaceted truth in its essential, oneness. This is explained excellently in the *Upanishads*, which say that, salt when mixed with water becomes a part of it, and the whole water becomes salty, yet the salt preserves its essential self in extended form. The salt is not noticed, only water is. An organisational researcher therefore, must.
- not force his views on organisations.
- let feelings be sensitive to others.
- live through people's lives and experiences.
- develop bonds of feeling.
- notice an essential unity and ignored and trace its pattern.

- not ignore dark corners, unpleasant and ignored events and persons.

Yeti: In short, it means that in order to research into behaviour of yaks, you should live like yaks. Ha! Ha!

Nachiketa: I may quote here an interesting piece of advice given by a Chinese Master on how to paint bamboos; "study bamboo for ten years; become bamboo yourself, and target about bamboos then start painting bamboos." A state of identification is essential in the development of insights.

Yeti: But does that mean that you cannot study organisations without really being part of them.

Nachiketa: Not necessarily. Living with organisations gives you a certain exposure. What is needed is exposure, but this could be missed, if one does not develop feeling and only relies on intellectual and abstract tools.

Yeti: How can you define your 'feel' and convey it to others? It is a highly subjective tool.

Nachiketa: It is subjective. So is an interview. The method of OPU involves *inter alia*:

- developing feeling as suggested earlier.
- using EUT (Employee Understanding Technique).

Yeti: That only sounds like some more jargon.

Nachiketa: Every new thing is not a product from vacuum. It has really evolved. Creativity comprises in finding connections amongst hitherto unconnected things. Most of the time the connections are imperceptible or undefined. A label is needed to define such connections.

Yeti: Let us understand this jargon precisely.

Nachiketa: Yes, let us. We must keep in mind that:

- Organisational Psychounity, is a system of understanding and improving organisations. Based on research, it regards a high degree of integration as essential for effectiveness of organisations. All organisations have an essential, common spirit, i.e., their mission and values. This is reflected in their shared norms and goals, called culture. The corporate culture is an indicator of the Psychounity and the Corporate Soul. OPU advocates an understanding of this unifying spirit and common perception of truth of making organisations effective. This is the school of self-realisation of organisations.
- Feelings, truly natural and free, are unifying links in an organisation. These represent emotional but sentient ways of discovering people. The road to understanding organisations is affection dynamics.
- Employee understanding techniques is a tool for understanding people.

Yeti: Why one more tool? Have you not enough of these?

Nachiketa: Not yet. It is very difficult to understand human beings. No method is complete or perfect. This technique, however, places more emphasis on the emotional aspect of people rather than their knowledge or skills.

Yeti: There must be other methods of this kind.

Nachiketa: Yes, Psychoanalysis too does so. But the essential difference lies in its approach of study of the adult patterns of relationships, rather than the infantile or primordial etiology of diseases. It does not deal with sickness, but rather helps in understanding people. Counselling is superficial, but OPU and EUT refer to dynamics of psychounity which provide clues. The emphasis is on discovering links' rather than only studying the aberrations or 'dislinks'.

Yeti: I think it too late in the night. The next time we meet, you should deal with this technique in detail.

Nachiketa: O.K., but let us have a drink before you go.

(Nachiketa goes to pour a drink. As he comes back he does not find Yeti in his chair. Nachiketa hastily gulps his drink and comes out of the tent. He discovers the foot-prints of Yeti on the snow leading up to the mountain peak. Strangely, there are delicate foot-prints along with his largish ones. Was it an illusion of duality?)

YETI SHUNS WORLDLY VICES

The abominable snowman might be a snowwoman since it has breasts and likes chickens. What is more interesting is chat it appears to be a teetotal. According to Indian mountaineer S. Wangyal, a Yeti approached his expedition in the Himalayas and later raided the kitchen tent, rendering it empty of chickens and all other foodstuffs. All that remained were bottles of beer and wine. Our abominable snowperson correspondent writes: This proves the Yeti is not human.

Bangkok Post, September 16, 1984

Chapter 5

Tools for Insights: EUT

The main intention is to come time and again to the nexus of feelings and linkage to gain insights into the emotional problem. The underlying assumption is that understanding these problems can improve relationships and their working.

7 Mantras for Managers

- ☆ *Explore feelings to study linkages and association of individuals in face to face dialogue, or in a group with one of the participations while others listen.*
- ☆ *Allow the individual to talk about self, work, associates, likes and dislikes.*
- ☆ *Understand people without trying to change them, or reform them.*
- ☆ *Probe perceptions—negative and positive—about self and others.*
- ☆ *Establish linkages and relatedness. Identify values.*
- ☆ *Express your concern and interest to understand people.*
- ☆ *Develop empathetic window to emotional psyche of people.*

Yeti: We were discussing EUT which we trust is for understanding the employees in organisations. Why do you call it EUT?

Nachiketa: Since the method of exploring the life of an employee is used in the organisational situation, it is called so. In fact, it only refers to a methodology to understand people and perhaps, you would be within your right if you call it PUT.

Yeti: Is it not simply a jugglery of words?

Nachiketa: It is not a jugglery of words, but looking at the same technique from the organisational point of view or from the point of general liking in society.

Yeti: Let us proceed with discussion. How do we actually use this method?

Nachiketa: EUT is basically an interview technique in which one person explores the feelings of another, especially to study his linkages with a view to understand him.

Yeti: Surely there must be many ways of interviewing?

Nachiketa: There are. But here we are using interview as a method to draw out relevant information from an employee. This method also attempts to cull out information for various other purposes. As I stated earlier, psychoanalysis is meant to find out information relating to the earliest experiences of a person, with a view to trace the etymology of a disease and to cure it. The assumption in the methodology is that a linkage is disrupted somewhere in the earlier part of his life leading to a particular disease. But psychoanalysis is a very prolonged and slow method of understanding the cases of emotional maladjustment and EUT is a short interview to understand the feelings and linkages of a person. The differences between the two are:

- Psychoanalysis takes a long time; EUT takes between 30 to 60 minutes.
- Psychoanalysis traces the history of disease and explores the earliest experiences; EUT concentrates on outward behaviour and recent experiences.

Therefore, the purpose of psychoanalysis is to probe a person from his childhood and the purpose of EUT is to understand one's behaviour with a view to smoothen the process of day-to-day behaviour. When once people talk about themselves and their feelings connected with other people with whom they relate we can know them better. It is uncovering the process and pattern of related information of a human being; it is also finding out the degree of relationship.

Yeti: Does it mean the socialisation process of a man?

Nachiketa: Not necessarily, since the emphasis is not on the sociometric aspect of knowing the pattern of choice but on the strength of linkages and the feelings connected with those linkages. Here I may mention that there are some more methods like counselling. The essential difference between the counselling process and that of EUT is that in the latter the emphasis is not on solving the problem but on understanding it. EUT does not fix its attention on the achievements or failures but simply on the linkages and feelings for the purpose of understanding. It does not counsel. Let me give you the purpose of EUT:

What EUT Intends to do	What EUT does not intend to do
• Explore	Cure
• Understand	Evaluate
• Reassure	Problem Solving

Yeti: What is this understanding on which you have hinged your hopes?

Nachiketa: Understanding for the purpose of EUT involves:

- Appreciating problems
- Discovering strengths.
- Connecting oneself to others.
- Identifying values.
- Diagnosing feelings.
- Recognising links.

In short, this is the process of diagnosis of feelings and linkages.

Yeti: How do you really conduct this interview?

Nachiketa: It can be conducted in two ways:

- Individual-to-individual basis, or
- Group interviews conducted by the leader.

For the purpose of understanding employees, it is better to resort to individual-to-individual basis interviews rather than group interviews. The reason for this is the fact that people open themselves up more conveniently in privacy rather than in the presence of others. Moreover, it is possible to gain confidence and explore other personalities in individual interviews.

Yeti: Can you describe this?

Nachiketa: Some prerequisites of this interview are:

- Informality of atmosphere.
- Genuine concern for the feelings of others.
- Allowing employee to talk more at the time of interview.

- Asking relevant questions.

After a person is seated and after exchange of pleasantries, the interview goes along the following lines:

- What kind of work do you do?
- How do you spend your time?
- What type of person do you think you are?
- What type of feelings do you entertain about the people you know and how do they affect your behaviour and work? Can you think of reasons?
- Can you tell of some events which describe your feelings about the people?

Yeti: How do you get information from the employees by merely asking these questions?

Nachiketa: The questions may seem to be simple, but they are only meant to stimulate the persons. The main intention is to come time and again to the nexus of feelings and linkages to gain insights into his emotional problems. The underlying assumption is on understanding these problems. Through this, people can improve relationships and their working.

Yeti: There is a Chinese proverb that a picture is better than words and actions are better than a picture. It would be better if you illustrate the whole thing.

Nachiketa: O.K. Here is a sample interview.

SAMPLE INTERVIEW OF EUT

Interviewer: Now, Mr X we are going through the discussion solely for the purpose of improving my understanding of you. My objective is not to evaluate; it is simply to understand. This means that there is no need for you to be apprehensive about being frank. Answer as freely as you can; you are talking to a friend.

Q. The first question is: "What kind of a person, do you think, you are?"

A. The first thing that comes to mind is that, well, I am a person who holds strongly to certain professional values inculcated in me early in my professional career. Excellence in what I do; objectivity as far as it can be achieved, hard work, etc., etc.

The second important feature about me is that I am weak in human relationships. Not that I dislike people, but that I relate to people less. To cite examples:

(i) My wife's complaint is that I "live in my office" even when I am at home. This refers to two habits of mine (1) of carrying work home and doing it there, and (2) more importantly, my habit of ruminating over issues, problems or plans that relate to work. I spend long hours doing the second, even when I am at home. Thus, let us say I have a job to do, like preparing a research proposal or writing a research report. I keep thinking about it, whenever I can find time and then I get so deeply involved in thinking, I forget my surroundings, or, at any rate, am unresponsive to it. This gives rise to the second problem.

(ii) All my family members have a complaint that I am unresponsive. This is how it happens—I am deeply involved in thinking out a problem or about a report or research proposal and one of my family members comes to me and asks a question. Either, I don't hear them at all or give a monosyllabic answer which over time, they have learnt to recognise as mechanical. For instance, my younger son comes and asks permission to go out and play (when his mother has told him to study) and I say, "Yes, Yes". These days, they also make fun of me, but that stage has come after considerable heartburns, as usual.

(iii) A third feature is that while I am miserly in being communicative with the family, I am quite communicative—almost voluble when outsiders come. My family is quick to note the contradiction, with the inevitable consequences.

Q. Have you been like this all the time?

A. For most of my life, yes, but not all the time. For instance, my sociability towards outsiders, if I remember correctly, is something I acquired, or let me put it, this way—I quite deliberately developed around the age of 28 or 29.

Oh! that brings me to another of my important characteristics—my sense of independence. For as long as I remember, I have been a very independent person in the sense that I won't depend upon other people's opinions. If A comes to me and tells me something about B, I simply would not pay any attention. My attitude is: I can make up my own mind, I don't need your help. This is how I justify my attitude. God has given me two eyes and two ears and other sensory equipment to know the world around me. No doubt, when I use them to know the world, I might err. But it is a single error. On the other hand, if I depend upon another person's eyes, ears, and senses, there is always the possibility that the other is in error. And, then, what I commit is a double error; his error compounded by my error in depending upon his view. Aren't single errors better than double errors, so to speak?

Up to the age of 28, this sense of independence on my part has landed me frequently in trouble. How? A friend comes and talks to me about another friend. I bluntly cut him short, saying "I don't want your opinion; let me make up my mind myself. There is no end to the number of enemies I made this way, until the age of 28 when I was fed up with the turn events were taking and decided to be less blunt. When I began to practise the new way assiduously, along came my "sociability" and it has stayed put ever since.

That is one change, I notice, which says I was not always like this, but there is a more fundamental change that took place around the age of six. Up to the age of six, I recall, I was the epitome of—what I know today—bubbling with life. At six, a radical change came and I became the exact opposite of what I was before.

Q. Was there anything particular that prompted this change?

A. Generally, let us say, the pressure of environment-pressures from father, mother, etc. Ah! yes, specifically it was this:

In those days, in my part of the country, it was customary to have your ears pierced (like you do with girls even today), even for boys. Actually, this is a ceremony preceded by *puja*, etc. The uncle presides over the ceremony, i.e., does ear-piercing.

Now, my elder brother's ear-piercing ceremony had taken place two years ago and he had been wearing earrings. I had been earnestly looking for the day when I would be putting on similar earrings. But when the day came, it was a disastrous disappointment.

There were no earrings. This was a terrible blow to my ego-my conception of myself as a lovable individual fell like nine pins. Soon, whether because of my uncle's lack of expertise, or for other reasons, my ears began to swell. They stayed swollen for quite a few days. But that swelling had a positive outcome; it helped me save face before others, who would otherwise torment me with the fact that I had no earrings. Looking back upon it, I suspect, the whole thing was psychosomatic in origin. The deflated ego never seemed to have recovered! Though my constant wish and endeavour ever since has been to enliven that part of me which had shrivelled under the impact of that rejection.

Q. Who are the people you are drawn towards?

A. There are exactly two—Dr K to whom I owe that what I am today and the venerable Mr K who is one of the most revered literary figures today.

You know Dr K? Had it not been for this venerable lady, I would not be where I am today—passable expert in Human Relations—and ironically enough, had it not been for her, I would have risen far higher than where I am. A contradiction? Exactly, this is what our relationship is.

She was (virtually) the Director of the Institution where I was a minor functionary and yet she was the one who inspired me to take on the study of Human Relations and change into the academic line where

I have attained a fair measure of success in the last 15 years or so.

Coming to Mr K he is my first cousin, though, up to the age of 29 or so, I am not sure I had set eyes on him. He is 10-12 years older to me, left home after some Sanskrit studies at the end of his primary schooling only to surface, after a decade or so as a D. Litt. in the regional language and authorship of a good deal of popular poetry. The ensuing years saw him partake of politics and a good deal of writing finally to settle down exclusively in the pursuit of literature. An intellectual giant of almost legendary fame, he is aid to know 14 languages, including Tamil, Hindi and English. Over the years, he earned greatness for himself as a poet, critic, essayist, playwright, editor; academy award winner, and so no.

In my adolescence and early youth, this Mr K whose face I could not clearly recall had remained my model. My attempts to model after him took me into literature and 'poetry quite deeply—so much so that by the age of 25, like all adolescents, I was trying my hand at poetry writing. Even today, I think, this Mr K has not lost his hold on me.

Q. What do you recall specifically about these two relationships?

A. That is the funniest part of the story. Both these relationships were heavily tinged with ambivalence right from the inception.

Q. What do you mean by ambivalence?

I will explain. Let us take Dr K first. I have already hinted at the gulf between us in terms of status. But she had somehow taken a fancy to me, I mean in the professional sense—and, I think, was keen to see me grow and develop in my career. Though I understood as much, I did not like the way she went about it—which I then defined to myself as "taking over". Now this idea of someone "taking me over" (even with the best of intentions) was abhorrent to me. (My sense of independence, I suppose). These minor dissatisfactions, however, had not broken the peace between us.

That peace was broken by another event which I think was the crucial event that determined our relationship. But before I come to that event, a little bit of history.

Until six months ago, I was taking care of a department in the organisation quite independently. Then, a young fellow, an America-returned, was appointed above me, as in-charge of the department. I rebelled—and rebelled so ferociously that I simply kept the fellow out of the department.

At First, everyone including Dr K looked upon the scene with condescending amusement. They tried to rain me with good-humoured amusement. I resented it and intensified my destructive psychological warfare against the newcomer. Finally, time came for a short training programme at M (a hill station) and all of us—myself, Dr K the new chap and several others left together for the hill-station.

The first day of the programme was a short orientation session where various teachers explained various aspects of the forthcoming course. It was Dr K's role to explain the methodology of the course. I sat there as the orientation programme went on. The new chap wasn't there.

Next morning, the new chap, Dr K and myself met at breakfast. Dr K asked "How did you (that is, me) like yesterday's programme?" and before I had time to answer she turned to the new chap and asked "tell me first, how did you like the programme." The new chap—a bundle of confusion because of my psychological warfare—mumbled at the end of which, Dr K turned to me and asked "Now, how did you like yesterday's programme?"

I was fuming with rage and I was ready with my answer even before she asked the question. I answered:

> "I think, the course methodology should have been explained to the class."

Dr K literally jumped out of her chair (and I think, I read admiration in her eyes).

Let me explain that when Dr K asked me the question and without waiting for my answer turned to the new chap with the same question I interpreted it as an attempt at manipulating me. In other words, most subtly, Dr K was sending me a message that the new chap was No. I and now I was No. 2. I admired her subtlety but, at the same time, I resented her manipulation. My admiration for her is responsible for edging me on to where I am today professionally, my resentment against her manipulative attempt kept our later relationship (lasting about 3 years) literally at the 'cat-and-mouse' level.

Let me digress here a little and tell you about my hatred of manipulation. The relationship between me and Dr K thereafter became quite well-known in the organisation an many were the do-gooders who were trying to put it on a more healthy plane. Here is one such incident.

He was our Administrative officer. I had gone to him for some business and in an awesome reverential tone, he said:

"Do you know, Dr K is writing a book?"

Now, I knew Dr K was writing a book. Her secretary often used to tell me about it. He also used to say, "Look, I am typing this for the fourth time" and so on.

I didn't like what he said. To me it was a naked attempt to influence me—to change my opinion of Dr K who was engaged in the great' task of writing a book! And I wanted to register my displeasure at this crude attempt at manipulation. So I said:

"Yes, but to be more precise, you should say, Dr K is writing a book ten rimes over."

He was greatly surprised and amused and by the time I returned to my seat, there was a lot of commotion in Dr K's room. Apparently she had got the news. That shows, how strongly I resent being manipulated.

Strangely enough, my only meeting with Mr K my cousin ended on the same ambivalent note. I went to his house in another city. He looked to me very indifferent. Though politely, I left soon, quite angry at his indifference and have never tried to see him again. Yet he continues to be my model. Now, look at the contradiction! The same individual admired and hated—the same event generating admiration and hatred.

Q. What are the kind of people you dislike?

A. There are very few people for whom I have unqualified dislike-though to most people I may be said to have an attitude of indifference. I remember one character. This chap was 'colourless' to say the least. He has no abiding interest in life, no avocation. Apart from the daily grind of doing one's work, earning money and living out a life, he had no interests. So, if you have met him twenty times, twenty times you would have listened to the same droning conversation, devoid of humour, devoid of novelty, devoid of any positive quality. He simply repelled me and whenever I could I avoided meeting him.

There was one more thing about him; total insensitivity to the listener as he continued with his unending drone!

Q. Have you tried to analyse your attitude towards Dr K? It was both admiring and destructive at the same time!

A. Your analysis is very correct. It was admiration and destructive hostility, both equally intensive. But I don't see anything beyond it. From my knowledge of psychology I would say, it was my Oedipus complex surfacing. But beyond that I know nothing Perhaps, I would never know.

Nachiketa: What do you think about this Interview?

Yeti: It seems to me that the man in EUT was articulate enough. I don't think this is true of everyone and this could not happen in interviewing ordinary workmen.

Nachiketa: I agree with you. The person being interviewed is a researcher and a writer.

Yeti: Do you find this EUT serving any useful purpose; what insights have you derived from these?

Nachiketa: After this interview, I started understanding him more in spite of the fact that I had worked with him for two years without knowing his background. EUT, leads to discovery of people, their strengths and problems.

Yeti: What have you discovered?

Nachiketa: From this EUT interview the interviewee emerges as a highly work-committed person who is motivated to achieve excellence in his own work. He is however, very complex in the sense he is constantly suffering from a psychological feeling of sibling rivalry firm his childhood. If you see in the above interview, what has happened to him in childhood has again been repeated later on. All the same it also shows that the man can achieve a lot if he is given recognition. It also shows that he is not capable of being a leader in an organisation, but he can excel in the type of work which involves research or writing.

What can be derived from this interview is that he has very few linkages. It also shows that his affection is linked to very few people. He is not capable of giving his feelings to a larger groups or many people. The leader on the other hand will have to develop feelings which can be linked to innumerable persons. He has also to be a person whose linkages are varied and wide.

Yeti: How can you substantiate it? It may be a purely subjective view.

Nachiketa: At the time to this interview, I had two observers, whose report is given below:

REPORT OF OBSERVER I

The whole interview was based on the following questions:

- What kind of a person do you think you are?
- Who are the people you feel drawn towards?
- Who are the people that you feel withdrawn from?
- Can you remember the specific events which drew you or withdrew you from these people?

Other probing questions were also asked.

Apart from being willing and work-oriented the interviewee seems to be a detached person especially where his family is concerned. He also seems to be a stubborn person as once he forms an opinion whether positive or negative about a person whatever may happen he sticks to his opinion and generally is not taken up by other people's views. The interviewee also suffers from a kind of fear that a person of authority might take him over and this he presents. He also seems to be jealous of others superseding and applies all tactics to curtail it. Through this interview the main objective of finding out the linkages and dislinkages of the person concerned were fulfilled.

The interview was simple and very probing and led to a greater understanding of the interviewee in addition to the interviewee having a greater awareness of self. It made us aware of how and why he behaves in a particular situation. One caution is that while applying this technique to other people one needs to make the interview more simple and more probing questions need to be asked.

REPORT OF OBSERVER II

Some Observations:

- The interviewee is very work oriented. Most of his experiences (quoted) centre around work and the effects due to his involvement in work.
- He seems to be an introvert. Does not care much for

a social life. However, he is more communicative with people he is working with.

- Thinks very often. In his own words, 75 per cent of his effort is done mentally. He is so involved in thinking that he forgets the immediate present.
- Does not seem to understand and hold strong family units.
- His self predominates and is not able to take in other's opinion. He cannot take in a newcomer superseding him and, in fact, he manipulates the situation to show his value. He also cannot tolerate being ignored at any place.
- Having admiration and hatred for the same person who has impressed him the most is distinctive. Both the meetings have ended with a sad note—is it that he expects too much from these individuals or else is very sensitive himself?
- Likes variety and humour in people.

  The interviewer seemed to enquire the attitude of the interviewee from three distinct aspects:

  - through perceptions of self
  - through perceptions of positive others
  - through perceptions of negative others

The other questions were of probing nature intended to go deeper and increase understanding of his views. This particular interview was very lucid, the questions well understood. Probably the respondent being a man of behavioural science was able to give concrete experiences.

Yeti: While I agree that in this case you can talk on various things, and a patterned interview could be better in understanding the human being rather than one without clear purpose, the question still remains as to how really it goes with the people who are not so articulate.

Nachiketa: I agree. It does not follow the same pattern of EUT as seen by us and it can vary with people. It depends on the interviewer to adjust according to the needs. Here I will give you an example of EUT with a very low paid workman, who is very different and much simpler.

ANOTHER EXAMPLE OF EUT

Mr S: What work are you doing?

Mr D: I am working as a despatch clerk in the despatch sectiol

Mr S: Why do you think you are doing it?

Mr D: I don't know. I got this job so I do it. May be to earn my living.

Mr S: What are your problems?

Mr D: So many. There is no system of work. My boss is always busy. He never has any time for me. There are promotions.............................

Mr S: If work is boring, what is interesting to you?

Mr D: My friends, I like to do union work: it helps me to do useful things.

Mr S: What type of person are you?

Mr D: I don't know.

Mr S: Who are the people you spend time mostly with?

Mr D: I think I spend time with my colleagues.

Mr S: Outside work?

Mr D: Mostly I am at home.

Mr S: Who are at home?

Mr D: None.

Mr S: You live alone?

Mr D: No, I have my brother living with me.

Mr S: What does he do?

Mr D: He doesn't do anything.

Mr S: Why? He is not studying?

Mr D: To tell you the truth, he is mad. He shouts, becomes violent. Sometimes (Pause) I have to be awake whole night.

Mr S: How do you manage this?

Mr D: What to do? One has to face one's fate. He has been like this for the last 3 years since my mother died. Since then he has been like this. I have not even married for his sake. I have to live with him.

Mr S: Why don't you send him to a mental asylum?

Mr D: No, I can't. It is costly. Moreover I cannot part with him.

Mr S: Are you giving him any treatment?

Mr D: No. Earlier I took him to Agra. But they gave him very inhuman shocks. I can't let him be subjected to such painful experiences.

Mr S: These days psychologists can help you. There are doctors who may treat him through less painful means.

Mr D: If there are, I'd try,

Mr S: Do so and keep me informed. Thank you.

Nachiketa: Above is an example of a very short elementary EUT.

Yeti: What does it show? I think it is just Chit Chat.

Nachiketa: May be but what it really tells you is a story of the tragedy of a man. If you know it you can deal with him better.

Yeti: How does it help?

Nachiketa: In this case, you will be surprised that his boss who was working with him for a decade did not know about his sick brother. Many a time this man came late. He was inattentive and sleepy. When I told his boss the story, he could appreciate his problems better.

Yeti: Did it change him?

Nachiketa: Yes, to some extent. His talk with me established a special link between him and me. Many a time I met him later and enquired about his brother. It made him not only feel better but also I found a look in his eyes as if he said "You know me." To me, he was kind and good too. Our perceptions of each other changed. Now I didn't find him an unruly union official or a bored and sleepy worker but as a suffering person, a lonely brother who was sacrificing himself for the sake of another. None had discovered him.

Yeti: I think I must try EUT on my Yak. But whenever I look into his eyes I know what he wants. So he does about me. We understand so much about each other without talking about it.

Grrrrr. A plane hovered above them in the sky. Perhaps a mountain flight carrying tourists, who wanted to have a glimpse of Sagarmatha. The day was clear. White clouds sneaked behind the mountain tops. The sky was azure blue like a deep ocean. Nachiketa wondered, was the deep sea above us, or where Everest stood or within us? Yeti was gone for another EUT with his YAK. Nachiketa gazed and could only shout at the mountain peaks. 'Where are you?' And there returned an echo. 'Where are you?' And again there returned an echo. 'Where are you?' Perhaps Yeti was mocking at Nachiketa or was it an echo of EUT?

Chapter 6

Of Mission and Objectives

No organisation can function effectively with such deflected aim. The team functions best when it shares the same mission. Integration is the outcome of such common spirit.

7 Mantras for Managers

- ☆ *Analyse and synthesise the activities of an organisation to understand it. Such an understanding would lead to reorientation.*
- ☆ *Set highest priority and mission in your projects as well as functioning of an organisation. Relate projects, targets and strategies to the mission.*
- ☆ *Use MOKSHA as a tool to analyse and synthesise.*
- ☆ *Define long-term and short-term orientation to link day-to-day actions contributing to the highest mission.*
- ☆ *Achieve greater integration by clearing the strategic direction of the organisation.*
- ☆ *Clear the confusion created by deflected mission or inverted mission.*
- ☆ *Answer why, what, when, how, where and how in terms of MOKSHA.*

Yeti: So here we are. Darjeeling is situated on the southern side of the Himalayas. How is it that Kanchanjunga and Sagarmatha are as beautiful when we look at them from Nepal, as when we watch them from Darjeeling. On both sides we see the same mountains.

Nachiketa: It is like two sides of a coin.

Yeti: This is how you are one and yet you are two.

Nachiketa: It is a very clever remark. Indeed, it is a symbolic representation of psychounity. You see variety from all dimensions but you are aware of its fundamental oneness. What makes it Kanchanjunga is not one side or other, but all sides. Kanchanjunga is there too and here too.

Yeti: How do we really relate it to your obsession of 'Organisationology'?

Nachiketa: It is the basic theme. Each organisation pursues a basic and fundamental purpose. That one purpose is supreme but it can be reached through divergent routes and sides. The summit is the mission and its flanks are objectives.

Yeti: Mission and objectives could be the same. Why should we separate summit and flanks?

Nachiketa: I agree ultimately they constitute one whole but we are following both methods of synthesis and analysis to understand it. Especially whey we want to break down a whole into parts, it is with a purpose to evolve steps and operationalise planning. It is a choice of one over others and priorities, which determine the mission-objectives exercise. Let me explain it with a Mount Everest analogy.

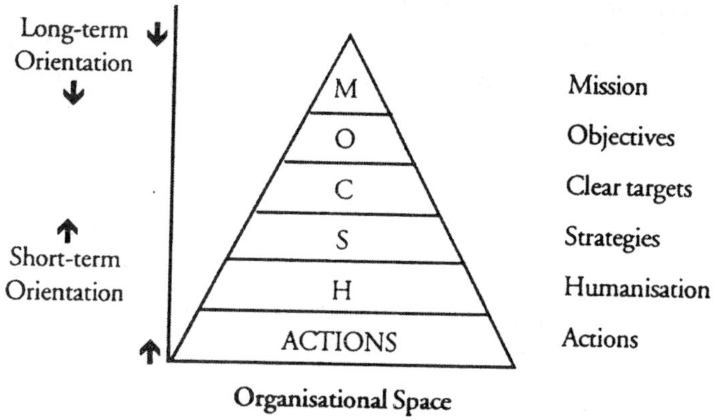

As you will see from the pyramid, the highest priority is mission. Everything else is below it. Summit is the final point. Successful explorers want to reach it, but they have to go through various stages. Final aim, however, continues to goad them. Those who settle down at earlier stages remain below the summit. Similarly current problem in the organisational world is that mission is either forgotten or remains clouded. Managers continue to grapple with lesser priority areas without linking them with the highest priority, the mission.

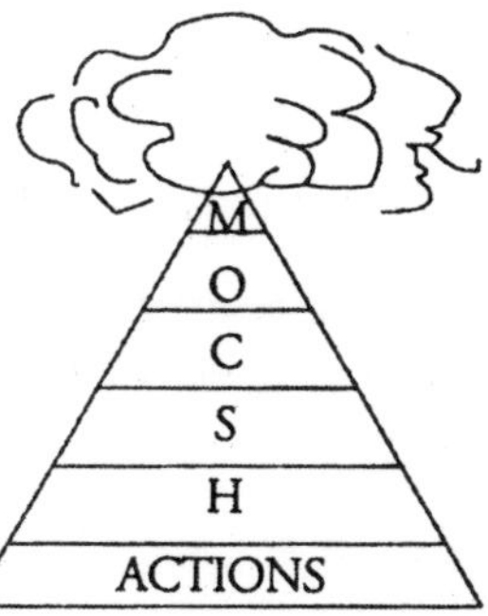

Yeti: One could be as happy as Yak, living at lower strata as it is quite cold at the top.

Nachiketa: But remember Yak's mission is not to reach the highest point whereas mountaineer's is. If the mission is below the summit then we redraw this as in the diagram.

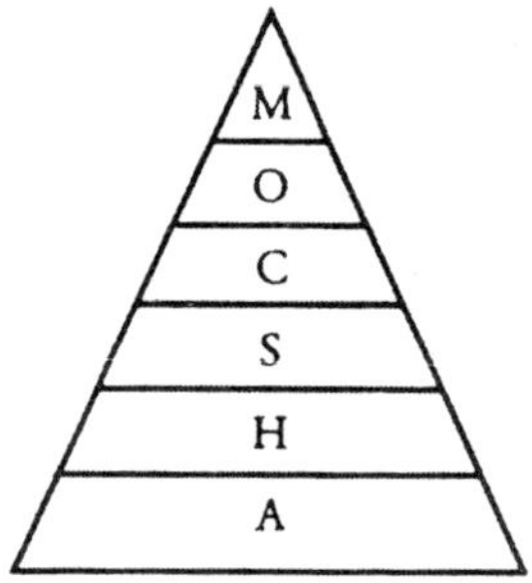

Mission Yak's Target in his Mission Climber's Mission

The most important point, therefore, is to determine your mission and then in relation to it work out other steps. Mission can change and in accordance with change, the rest of the steps also change. The greatest stumbling block in organisational effectiveness is confusion of mission, lack of prioritisation of various steps and inability of an organisation to work as an organic whole to achieve its aim.

Typical comment of the employees of an ineffective organisation is "We don't seem to know where we are going."

Yeti: Will you elaborate on what is mission?

Nachiketa: Mission is a long-term purpose. It is the highest value for the organisation. It is a touchstone for all the values.

Characteristics of mission are:

- It is long term;
- It is an answer to 'Why' of existence of the organisation;

- It is normative, representing values;
- It is supreme and everything else needs to be attuned to it;
- It serves to integrate the organisation;
- It directs rather than drives the organisation.

Let us now understand how confusion takes place. In a plant producing drugs we held a MOCSHA workshop. Before doing the exercise we asked the participants to identify the mission. You will be surprised to know that divergent perceptions emerged. (See Illustration A)

- To bring down drug prices.
- To produce drugs on a large scale.
- To make profits.
- To meet social objectives.
- To indigenise the drug on a large scale.
- To act as check on exploitative tendencies of multinationals.
- To develop drug technology.

Obviously the comprehension of Mission is confused. No organisation can function effectively with such deflected aim. The team functions best when it shares the same mission. Integration is the outcome of such common spirit. After we explained our MOCSHA Organisational understanding system, the same participants worked out the following definition of mission and objectives.

MISSION

To produce quality drugs for people at reasonable prices and contribute to achieving self-reliance in the country.

OBJECTIVES

- Maximise the production/capacity utilisation.
- Improve technology.
- Develop human resources optimally.
- Reduce production costs.
- Indigenise the production.
- Earn fair profits.
- Help in social and economic well being of a community.

Yeti: How can one differentiate Mission and Objectives?

Nachiketa: One simple way is to prioritize the objectives and aims. The highest aim is the mission. One must, therefore, frequently ask 'which is more important?' Moreover mission links organisational objectives to a wider sphere of society. Mission is not an amalgam of all objectives but only one or a few highest valued ones.

Yeti: Having understood it, I think I should do something about my mission since I have no organisation.

Nachiketa: True. As an organisation needs a mission so does an individual. There are plenty of *dishaheen* (directionless) people as there are organisations. One needs to draw one's mission. In Indian philosophy, there is considerable deliberation on *Moksha* or *Nirvana*. The highest value of life of a man is *Moksha*, or the freedom in enlightenment. Next comes *Dharma*, (performance of role and duty) followed by *Artha* (economic activity) and Kama (delight of senses).

Yeti: It is clear that four ultimate values were prioritised 2000 years back. But can one achieve the highest value without realising the lower ones? Or, are there short-cuts?

Nachiketa: Let us understand the instrumentalities of

achieving the highest values. Indian philosophy lays down normative way of life in which a man begins his life with self-control and discipline to learn his role or duty. He passes through a period of family life showing delight of senses and securing means to lead a secure life.

Freud spoke of libido and sex only in the nineteenth century in Europe. But in Indian philosophy this important aspect of life had its rightful place much earlier. The libido is treated as a secular issue without importing with it the burden of guilt which we notice in modern times.

Nevertheless it is possible to attain the mission without realising all the objectives fully. Objectives are not conditions for achievement of mission but only subsidiary aids or intermediary goals. But the fact remains that an integrated approach is more smooth and less strenuous.

An individual may not realise the value of *Karma* or *Artha* and still achieve complete freedom. Qualitatively the state of that freedom will be much different and strenuous from that of one who has fulfilled these. In fact, *Moksha* itself is pure feeling of bliss and it needs development of intense awareness. Similarly, in an organisation you may partly attain the mission even without fuller development of capacities or generating adequate surplus. But complete realisation of mission needs optimum goal or objective achievement. In the example quoted by us, a company may achieve partly the mission of self-reliance and yet make losses. But obviously it thwarts complete realisation since it would be dependent and not able to grow or expand. Its realisation would be limited.

Yeti: Let me now seek my release from you. Indeed, complete freedom . . . . . .

It seemed clouds enveloped them. They could not see each

other. It started raining heavily. A cyclone could have caused this sudden downpour. Yeti could not be seen. Nachiketa wished he could tell Yeti that complete freedom is a matter of intense realisation and not running away. Rain and clouds prevented the discourse. Nachiketa did not know whether Yeti was still waiting for his answer or not

Chapter 7

Diagnosing the "Organisational Unconscious"

Normally, .we manage organisations by understanding them through the eyes of pro-active people, or as management would say, desirable people. We dislike and avoid looking at organisations through 'undesirable people'. However, such a classification is artificial and exposes the bias of the leadership. The reality of an organisation must be understood in its totality. We must have an accurate and inter-subjective picture of the 'whole' and not a 'part'.

7 Mantras for Managers

- ☆ *Observe dark corners of an organisation through people who are not pro-actives and are ignored.*
- ☆ *Understand an organisation in totality and not as seen in a part of it.*
- ☆ *Understand organisational blind spots by using useful pictures of reality as seen by non-contributing people.*
- ☆ *Transform such people to involve actively in the organisational mission by understanding them.*
- ☆ *Diagnose the organisation by analysing performance, absenteeism, needs of members, literature and its folklore.*
- ☆ *Re-build the picture of an organisation after diagnosis and unleash the energy of unused people.*
- ☆ *Perform the reforming process with an attitude of a professional doctor rather than with a view to punish people.*

Yeti: You 'civilised' chaps are funny; you create complications and then find ways and means to simplify them. Is it not an endless game off utility? Why the hell do you need instruments to gain insight into organisations?

Nachiketa: I think we have already tried to deal with the issue when we started our dialogues. Anyway, Civilisation is a product of sublimation. It is a creative dimension of libidinal urges to the cause of progress.

Yeti: Yes, we did speak about progress. But your goals and missions are mere words. They are like bubbles. You prick them and nothing is left. If nature causes a catastrophe, you come back to where you started from. You act like a spider weaving a web entangling itself in it. Is that progress?

Nachiketa: I do not disagree with your point of view. One can view life and civilisation from either of the two ends of a scale. I can explain this process of which the world is enamoured, in terms of an analogy. Take, for example, a child playing with sticks, stones and sand. He has two choices. He may merely gaze at everything and do nothing. Or he may make small huts, homes, draw shapes of rivers in the sand and make various forms. Almost all children will follow the second choice. Why? Because man has an urge to create. There is immense joy in this process of creation. Have you seen a child overjoyed at making a small home out of given material? Have you noticed the unrepressed joy of accomplishment? The same is true of all of us. Of course, you can argue that the child's activities are futile and he can leisurely gaze and enjoy, but you cannot deny that there is beauty of creation.

Civilisation, with all its shackles and discontent, is an outcome of a creative process. Its complexity and tension render it an agony, but its advancement and refinement are creative jobs. The present day organisations are ingredients of this process of civilisation and culture.

Yeti: OK. Even if we do have these organisations, why do we need to invent tools to understand them?

Nachiketa: Again, it is the same creative process. You cannot advance without becoming aware. You have an urge to know, understand and make. Today I will describe to you another tool of knowing organisations. The tool relates to, what I would like to call, studying the 'organisational unconscious'.

Yeti: Is it another new name? Something unknown?

Nachiketa: Yes. It is something much less known or even discussed by the organisational researchers. If one scans through literature, one would observe a great deal of attention paid to 'high flyers', 'talent', and 'competent managers'. Rarely does one know enough about 'inefficient people', the 'passive lot', 'failures', 'problem employees' and who I would like to call, organisational delinquents.

Yeti: But why 'unconscious'. They are known and then discarded.

Nachiketa: The very fact that they are discarded shows that they are not in the range of the 'conscious choice' of leaders. Since they are not liked, the natural tendency is to shy away from them, ignore them or forget them. Organisations would like to put them away from their ambit of operation. In practical life we choose people like this for attention in organisations.

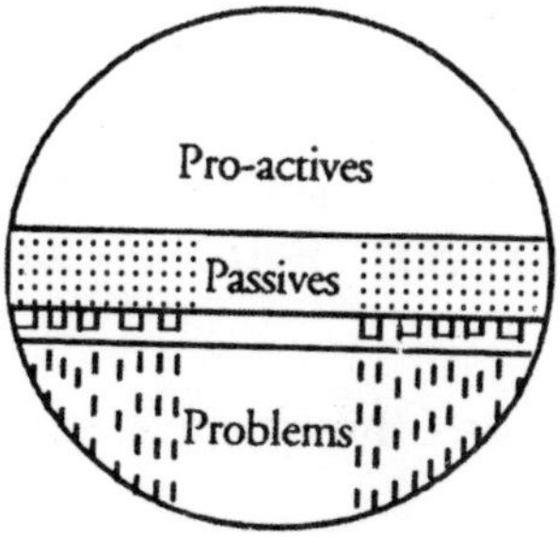

A psycho-map of organisational conscious

It is the bottom line which can sometimes turn the organisational destiny. But leaders of organisations shun them. They are driven towards the organisational unconscious. But what must be kept in mind is that 'passives' and 'problems' are not quiet. They are active towards objectives and goals of their own. While transforming them to contribute to your organisation objectives, something very significant for bringing about organisational change, the process begins by identifying them. Not by isolating them, but involving them in the process. Let us first try to diagnose them as a means to understand organisations.

Yeti: Are we understanding them or organisations?

Nachiketa: Both. This is because the unconscious' are very valuable instruments to understand organisations. Normally we manage organisations by understanding them through the eyes of pro-active people, or as management would say desirable people. We dislike and avoid looking at organisations through 'undesirable people'. However, such a classification is artificial and exposes the bias of the leadership. The reality of an organisation must be understood in its totality. We must have an accurate and inter-subjective picture of the 'whole' and not a part'.

Another reason why they can provide useful clues to understanding of organisation is that they have 'their own truth', a non-sanctioned truth. The complete picture of an organisation is as much a result of perceptions of pro-active people, as that of the 'undesirable ones'.

Yeti: You mean to say one set of people say it is good, another set says it is bad. Then the complete picture is, indeed, confusing.

Nachiketa: No. It means the true picture is somewhere in between the good and bad. Where exactly it is, depends on many factors like:

- the range of perceptions of organisational unconscious and its strength and force.
- Interpretations, analysis and re-interpretation: the symbols and motives of question.
- Co-relation of perceptions with other data.

Yeti: Now you are building another case like that of the child and sand?

Nachiketa: Yes (laughs). I will explain. The discarded elements of the organisations can provide very valuable insights as they look at things differently. If a researcher uses their perceptions and responses, by using 3 points check list given above, he builds a better picture of reality. Simultaneously, the fact that we talk to these people, involves them in the mainstream.

Yeti: But how do we identify such people?

Nachiketa: By studying the following available information in each organisation.

- Record of performance.
- Record of absenteeism.
- Comments and remarks of the Senior Managers during discussions and sampled group observations.
- Published literature.
- Gossip and stories prevalent in the organisation (organisational folklore).

Yeti: All this may point to the existence of areas of darkness and to the fact that there are some nocturnal people who dwell in this darkness. What then?

Nachiketa: This is the diagnosis of the 'organisational

unconscious'. The next task is to unleash the energy of these unused people to organisationally meaningful objectives. The problem is that all such people who are either indifferent or ignored or shunned are not dead. They area highly active in their own way. Either they are working against the objectives of the organisations or for personal ends which do not relate to organisations.

Yeti: But why should one spend time and efforts on such a difficult assignment? Instead we should concentrate on proactive elements who would be too willing to get energised for useful tasks. In our search of the 'delinquents' we may come across criminals and such people cannot be converted to positive attitudes easily. An organisation is not an asylum for such delinquents.

Nachiketa: It depends on the culture and values of the country and the organisation. If the Western system of 'hire and fire' is acceptable, you may resort to cutting and scissoring. But in other cultures, it is a social obligation on organisations to restore damaged links to the extent possible. Where criminality is proved, you may proceed to perform surgery, but where lesser degree of problems exist, a rejuvenation could be possible. It is just like each home nurturing patients who could recover otherwise hospitalisation is inevitable.

Yeti: OK. How do you bring back these people to become pro-activists?

Nachiketa: The first step would be the identification of such people on the basis of indicators already mentioned by me. The second step would be the diagnosis of their problems. The third step will be the treatment of such people. Proper diagnosis of these people is in itself a treatment. We can extensively use the Employee Understanding Technique (EUT) to create links. But the problem in using EUT is that managers themselves have to be trained in using this technique. The basic assumption is that understanding these people leads to their forming a link with the organisational objectives.

In Japanese organisations, for example, every effort is made to involve all the people in organisational work and employees are not thrown out when not required. Similarly according to Indian philosophy it is believed that everyone has some virtue and it needs to be deciphered. Moreover sometimes people on the dark side of the organisations have a great deal of skill and energy. It is necessary to tap it.

Yeti: It is growing dark outside. Perhaps, we are also in the same dark corner. Let us run for another sunshine.

('Yeti sees his Yak in the distance and runs towards it, shouting sweet nothings. The sun is slowly going down behind the Sagarmatha. The edges of the mountains are lit bright. Nachiketa can clearly see the footprints of Yeti etched in the snow against the lengthening shadows. The Yak's hoofs mingle with Yeti's in the distance. Something dark seems to be enveloping Nachiketa too. He plods back to his camp reflecting on the sunny side and dark corners of life').

Chapter 8

Organisational Unconscious: Signs and Symbols

I think the laws of the underworld are different and we should understand these laws. In the underworld, 'ruthless self interest' is the highest motive. While diagnosing this segment of organisation, one should not forget this law.

7 Mantras for Managers

- ☆ *Understand organisations by diagnosing signs and symbols of unconscious.*
- ☆ *Identify people amongst pro-active who are inwardly operating against the organisational mission.*
- ☆ *Study signs of counter-productivity by analysing moon-shining activities contributing to the growth of self-interest at the cost of the organisation.*
- ☆ *Study absences, over-spending behavior, grant of favours, social contacts and wide fluctuations in decision-making.*
- ☆ *Adopt a researcher's approach to frame a hypothesis and test it.*
- ☆ *Differentiate between laws of the pro-actives and those in the underworld.*
- ☆ *Use eyes as the most sensitive organ: observe.*

Nachiketa: Last time we discussed the organisational unconscious. It was only to add another dimension to our understanding the organisation.

Yeti: Yes, we were caught between sunshine and shadows.

Nachiketa: Perhaps. But if you see the earth, it represents brightness and darkness in day and night phases. That makes it complete.

Yeti: Why go that far. I have not seen the earth. But I see how a snow-clad mountain is sunny on one side with dark shadows on the other side.

Nachiketa: That is the basic issuc. To know its complete reality and not confine ourselves to the visibility alone. Most of us live lives where there is only sunshine. We remain ignorant of the vast darkness which is an essential part of reality.

Yeti: So, OK

Nachiketa: Organisational unconscious is the dark side of the organisation. Last time I referred to employees, who are either neglected or discarded, as constituents of this unconscious. I wish to add to it by covering the entire activities, hidden from the management, of its people which are related to organisation but are not in the area of its focus or awareness. Such activities, may be of people who are not ignored or discarded, but are in the mainstream.

Yeti: That means everyone is in the realm of unconscious.

Nachiketa: Not necessarily. If we examine activities of the conscious-sphere men, there may be a small number who may be acting counter to the mission and objectives of the organisation. But this segment can be more damaging than the one which is in the unconscious sphere. They constitute the semi-conscious sphere of the organisation.

Yeti: I think it needs specification.

Nachiketa: Let us take a look at the following:

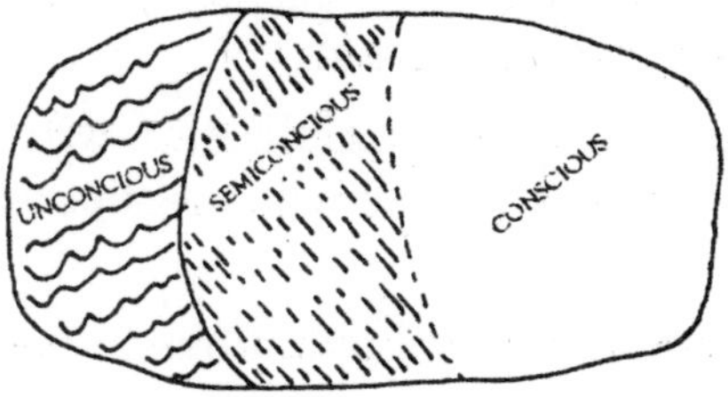

The activities of the inhabitants of the semi-conscious sphere can be:

- Engaged in another profession stealthily.
- Carrying information to competitors/rivals.
- Tarnishing the image of the organisation outside for personal gain.
- Engaged in making profit for oneself at the cost of organisational interest.

Yeti: But how can you say the people in unconscious sphere are not doing these things?

Nachiketa: I am not saying so. The only differentiation I am trying to bring to your notice is that while the unconscious sphere is identifiable and hence less harmful, the semi-conscious sphere is more difficult to identify and highly explosive.

Yeti: How to identify such people as they appear normal on face value?

Nachiketa: Some signs of semi-conscious sphere are:

- Numerous anonymous letters, telephone calls about activities of such people.

- Frequent absence from office.
- Over-spending/affluence not related to known sources of income.
- Grant of favours, concessions by them to undesirable or unscrupulous people.
- Contacts, meetings, socialisation with unscrupulous people or such people who are a potential source of problems.
- Wide variations or fluctuations in decision-making: very slow sometimes, very fast sometimes.

Yeti: Even if we identify such people, it is a matter of doubt and not reality. How do you establish their credentials or the lack of it?

Nachiketa: It is true that the identification based on the above tools is only tentative. But then one knows where to look and what to guard against. The second stage is to subject their activities and decisions to microscopic observations. It is bound to result in evidence or absence of it.

Yeti: It is like catching a thief. You expect your organisationology to become a crime detection science?

Nachiketa: It is very strange that all methods of reality testing are similar in basics. Take research. You have hypothesis. Then you start looking for proof through an experiment or observation and then you find one or fail to find one. So is the case of a medical man. He sees symptoms, frames a tentative diagnosis, conducts further tests and arrives at the final diagnosis for appropriate treatment. What do you do? You look at hoof marks of yak, infer that yak has gone in a particular direction, run after these marks. and find him. Sometimes you fail to find him by this method. Those marks turn out to be of some other animal.

Yeti: I don't think I make a mistake about hoof marks in the snow. I recognise them.

Nachiketa: How? First of all, you have known them well. Secondly, you have a long association with them. Thirdly, there are not too many confusing and similar signs. It, therefore, needs a good deal of experience to diagnose and identify such people. But the biggest problem in this area is your unfamiliarity with such people as contrasted to your familiarity with Yak. I know there are senior managers who used to say: you cannot understand a vicious mind, without being somewhat vicious yourself.

Yeti: I think it is rather unfortunate that you are teaching understanding organisations by making people vicious?

Nachiketa: I do not say that. But I think the laws of the underworld are different and we should understand these laws. In the underworld, 'ruthless self interest' is the highest motive. While diagnosing this segment of organisation, one should not forget this law.

Yeti: It is garbage. Why do we see all this?

Nachiketa: I agree with you that 'seeing' is an important but not the only means of knowing. Eyes are perhaps the most sensitive organ and hence the most revealing. But when only eyes are involved, it becomes a tricky situation. You know how eyes can falter and see a rope as a snake. Because signs and symbols are interpreted by mind. Eyes only transmit the image. The interpretation is subject to too many mental programmes. Hence the need to follow more than one cue approach to check and re-check the perception.

As Nachiketa looked around, he found Yeti missing. He shouted in the valley: "Yeti, Yeti, Yeti, where are you?" An echo greeted him: "Yeti, Yeti, Yeti, where are you?" And there was a long silence afterwards. Nachiketa was baffled.

Was it Yeti mocking at him or was it the echo of the valley? Nachiketa had a vague intuitive feeling that Yeti might return next day.

Chapter 9

Understanding Organisational Culture: Values

I agree it needs clarification. Need culture too implies value? But in my coining the phrase, I have differentiated between short-term and long-term goals. A need culture signifies urgency and in patterns it reflects speed and satisfaction in this case, therefore, values so chosen are of immediate concern rather than stable or futuristic concern.

7
Mantras for Managers

- *Develop organisational hierarchy of values rather than hierarchy of needs.*
- *Introduce clarity of roles and high performance of duty.*
- *Differentiate between highest values truth beauty and goodness as the ultimate springs of action and the mundane needs at physical and social planes.*
- *Bridge the existing gulf between cognitive practices and cognitive values to reduce hypocrisy and bring transparency in actions.*
- *Synthesise Western logic with Eastern emotionalism.*
- *Check short-term goals functioning counter to long-term ones.*
- *The final hierarchy of values is determined by duty, wealth, love and above all, enlightenment and freedom.*

Yeti: You have been talking a lot about values. We spoke earlier about Western culture. To me, there does not appear to be any distinction. All values must finally lead to the summit: the truth.

Nachiketa: I agree. But these days, the terms 'values', 'culture', 'organisational values' are so often being used loosely that it becomes necessary to clear these up.

Yeti: I too get a vague feeling. It is good to lay at rest this controversy.

Nachiketa: Yes. I spoke of end values, or ultimate values. You know these only consist of *satyam, shivarn* and *sundaram*, i.e., truth, beauty and goodness. There are of course, scores of other values, Indian philosophy also mentioned *dharma, artha, karma* and *moksha* as values. These too are values, but *dharma* and *moksha* are more fundamental than *artha* and *karma*. This hierarchy of value system has been created by our people. Whereas the West got obsessed by hierarchy of needs, we were always concerned with hierarchy of values. Values are more profound and perennial springs of action than needs.

Yeti: Sometimes I feel our needs shape values. Again, all food is not without value. Or, take money as a value, even accepted by Indians.

Nachiketa: Needs and values are interlinked but values lead the course. When I discussed with you the mission-objectives exercise and gave you hierarchy of objectives, I really wanted to demonstrate that the hierarchy of values is a directing force for all behaviour, especially leader-behaviour.

Yeti: When Buddha speaks of emptiness, or the Indian Vedantic system preaches *Maya*, where are your values?

Nachiketa: This ultimate analysis is only with a view to understand our insignificance and relatedness. We tend to feel different and attach too much value to self. Self is a part of the cosmos and the cosmos is a part of self. One who sees the whole cosmos in oneself and oneself in the whole cosmos, transcends these distinctions. He really gets the vision of unity in diversity. This was the phenomenon referred to by me as psychounity.

Yeti: Again, we seem to get to the top without crossing the plains and valleys. Let us analyse the organisational values.

Nachiketa: Thanks, indeed! (Pours Scotch for Yeti). Let us also consider our own organisational world. It is an inter-related micro-view. Attitudes reflect our day-to-day feelings towards various issues. We are not happy with the dictatorial boss. We don't like merit-based promotions.

These are attitudes, which do reflect values but are not values. Values reflect more durable clusters of attitudes. In fact, we can diagrammatise these as under:

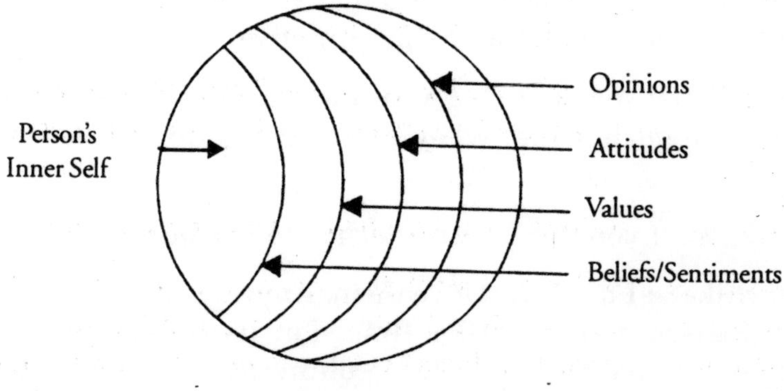

Beliefs represent larger groups of values internalised and, in many cases, unconscious. Values are deeper feelings towards norms. These are normative whereas attitudes need not be normative. Patriotism is desirable and hating a non-Indian may not be. The former is a value and the latter is an attitude. You may come across such non-Indians whom you may start liking also. You are agitated over the Sri Lanka issue. It is a matter of opinion, which is a transitory matter.

Yeti: (Yeti has gulped down three pegs). I think you are only creating unnecessary layers of distinctions. Who cares? Let it be opinion or value. Does it matter?

Nachiketa: The question is: which is more deep and the final determinant of behaviour. That is why, we talk of 'value culture', which is more a long-term affair than 'need culture'.

Yeti: But you are talking of need culture as if Westerner's are heathens. Am I a creature of need culture or value culture?

Nachiketa: You are beyond both. You see, when someone transcends needs and values, he lives a natural life like you.

Yeti: I am not pleased. But is that what you think I have done? Or, is it that I am living primitively?

Nachiketa: You are living a natural life. Even civilised man can live such a life, when attachments do not become prisons.

Yeti: Don't you think I am attached to yak or mountain?

Nachiketa: I think you love them. Anyway, this matter we will discuss some other time. Let us concentrate on organisational systems. Need culture refers to a tradition and pattern established in an organisation whereby satisfaction of needs of people becomes prime consideration of the group. Needs are unresolved tensions or states of disequilibrium. For example, hunger, thirst, sex and safety are all such basic needs. A man who moves primarily to satisfy these contributes to need culture.

Yeti: But there may be other than physiological needs, like social relations, love, etc.

Nachiketa: Socialisation, yes. But not love. Love is a value. It is intrinsic and has no other ends.

Yeti: It is funny! How can socialisation not be a value?

Nachiketa: Socialisation is meant to achieve a certain satisfaction, a social status, or ego enhancement. It is only a force impelling an organism towards some goal. Love is not. It is an end in itself.

Yeti: Love may also enhance ego or pleasure.

Nachiketa: No. If it only enhances ego or pleasure, it is not true love. Genuine feeling of love may cause pain or damage to ego but it is an end in itself. Values are desirable end states or goals, and not impelling factors to achieve some goals. A Western social scientist has referred to self-actualisation as the highest form of need. He is mistaken. Self-actualisation really is value, if it is desired in itself and not for other goals. The distinction between needs and values is to be made clear in terms of impelling forces and end states. For example, friendship is a need if it is meant for business relations, but a value if it is intrinsic.

Yeti: To me, it looks a jigsaw.

Nachiketa: Let us then differentiate between needs and values graphically.

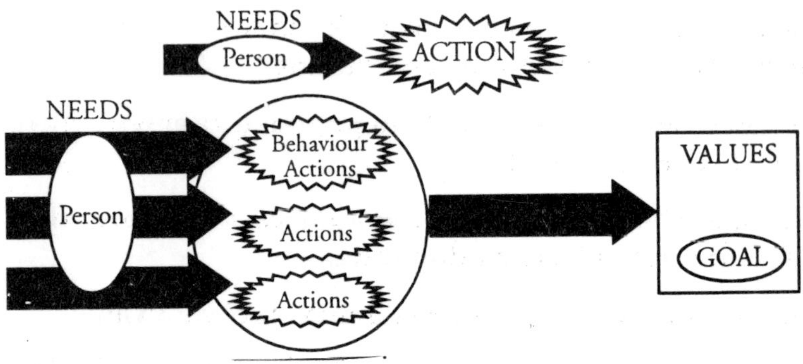

The needs impel a person to some action whereas values are goals, which direct or provide orientation to behaviour. All goals are values, or consist of some values for the person.

Yeti: In other words, goals are temptations.

Nachiketa: True goals have values and hence cause attractions. For example, let us think of a child of ten years.

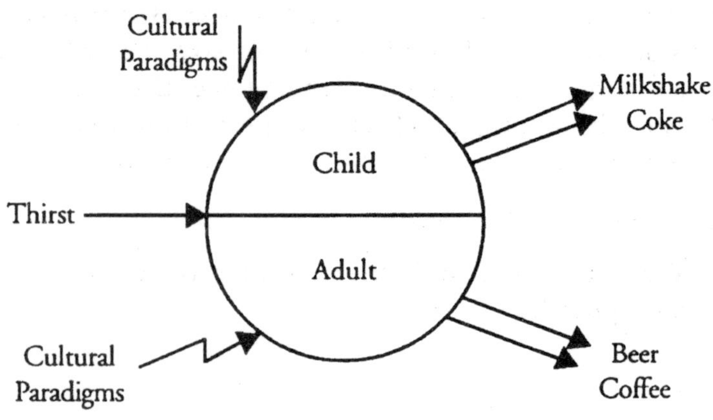

A child may select coke. An adult may select beer. This is an expected pattern of behaviour. When a child selects beer, it becomes unexpected. Why? Since it denotes departure from a cultural paradigm. As a child grows in a culture, he learns ways of choosing goals according to expectations of a culture. This is the effect of a culture, which really represents a common pattern of values and behaviour of a set of people acquired over a period of time.

Yeti: If all goals have values, then these are related to needs. How can we then differentiate between need culture and value culture?

Nachiketa: I agree it needs clarification. Need culture too implies values. But in my coining the phrase, I have differentiated between short-term and long-term goals. A need culture signifies urgency and in patterns it reflects speed and satisfaction. In this case, therefore, values so chosen are of immediate concern rather than stable or futuristic concern. A true Hindu is supposed to have learnt patience due to his concern for another life. Similarly, Buddhist; Jain or other eastern religions teach sacrifice of immediate gratification for future *moksha*. Patience, sacrifice, renunciation and long-term perspective is characteristic of an oriental mind. A typical Westerner is likely, at need level, to quench his thirst-and not fast to remain without water for days—to achieve enlightenment. A need culture, therefore, implies achievement of immediate goals rather than mission orientation built into value culture.

Yeti: If we see the typical portraits of an Eastern and a Western man drawn by you, we feel an Eastern man is ascetic but a Western man is eat-drink-and-be-merry type.

Nachiketa: In terms of caricature, yes. But more accurately, no. what is stated by me above is in reference to true Eastern (ancient) culture and not what prevails today. In fact, we suffer in India from an inversion of values. Let me describe it in a table:

TABLE 1

Cognitive Values	Practised Values
• Awareness of Mission and Values in Life	• Soft Work Culture
• Clarity of Roles and High Performance of Duty	• Regression of Trust Dimension and Role Ambiguity
• Self-sacrifice and Sensitivity to Others	• Short-term Gains and Emphasis on Self
• A Holistic Approach and Exploration of new Insights/Creativity and Continuous Learning	• Orthodox, Castism, Divisionalism and Resistance to Change/New Technology

Yeti: It is very funny indeed! First, you differentiate between two cultures. Then, you proceed to show that what you say is not true.

Nachiketa: The comparison I made was both on cognitive and conative planes. I have now introduced time element to show that reversal of values is the result of alien influences. In India, we have lost our identity and suffer from schizophrenia. At cognitive level, we still value the old values but in action we are just the opposite.

Yeti: Is it true of Indians or others too?

Nachiketa: It is true of the Indian sub-continent at least as far as my knowledge goes.

Yeti: But how do you come to this conclusion that a split exists?

Nachiketa: One can study the values by analysing popular arts which significantly influence the lives of people. Let us look at Indian movies. These represent the great cleavage. Almost all films eulogise true love, anti-materialism, truth, idealism, respect for parents, chastity of women, etc. Nevertheless, the analysis of film magazines depicting the lives of all these people, who represent our ideals, shows that in reality they practise just the opposite of it. Despite all celluloid sentimentalism, brazen materialism is the stark reality.

Yeti: But movies never represent life.

Nachiketa: I agree. This cleavage, in some degree, also exists in Western countries but its contours are blurred. In our case, the contrast is much more pronounced and dramatic. All differences are differences of degree when we talk of human values.

Yeti: Granted that this split exists, what do we do? Let it be?

Nachiketa: Split is the cause of strain in our society. It is also one of the important reasons of our under-productivity and ineffectiveness.

Yeti: It is a distant correlation.

Nachiketa: No. Take the question of credibility. In our society, it is at the lowest ebb, whereas in Western system, it is very high. In work relations organisational commitments are more honoured leading to a fair degree of reliability.

Yeti: Now I find you speaking highly of Western practices.

Nachiketa: There is no such things as universally good or bad in the two hemispheres. They are just like two parts of the brain—right and left-each with its own characteristics. Finally, a synthesis of the two could only lead to progress. As you will recollect, we discussed the discontents and virtues of civilization. The more we advance in industry and technology, the more we shall need the holistic outlook. The precision, meticulous planning and coordination of simultaneous multiplicity in operations will need a work culture close to Western rationalism and Eastern affection. The emerging profile of future organisations is replete with possibilities of combining two opposites in its ways of work.

Yeti: Let us continue with your 'split theory'.

Nachiketa: What I have tried to make is that the split is real and corrodes work culture. Organisations, therefore, have to prioritise our values. In fact, value represents a priority. It is the interrelationships of these and hierarchy which determine the framework of a work culture.

Yeti: How do we prioritise values? Even that would involve value judgement?

Nachiketa: It does. But we have some indications based on past experience, research and literature. Mission signifies the highest value.

Yeti: Why not objectives or targets?

Nachiketa: Because short-term goals should not function counter to the long-term ones. subordinate long-term ones, short-term interests to, we are destroying the future. It is natural. for man to preserve himself. If you drink too much and remain sick for days, you will prefer to drink in moderation unless you have a pathological problem. Here one is subordinating short-term interests to long-term ones. This is the basis of hierarchy which has been evolve by us. The mission represents the longest-term goal. In the time dimension, therefore, we have evolved a hierarchy of organisational values represented in tasks before an institution. We call it MOCSHA, which I have already explained to you.

Yeti: If this is hierarchy of values, where are your love, beauty or truth?

Nachiketa: This is only hierarchy of tasks but it also symbolises values in terms of priorities. Equally important is the question of style or how we really perform these tasks. It is the qualitative dimension of tasks. We may achieve our mission ruthlessly, or we may invoke love and affection to cherish it. It is our action or feeling which have values. Values are also normative. These depict desirable end states. (The conversation was disturbed by a group of climbers, who were talking loudly to each other about dangers ahead. Yeti disappeared. Perhaps to avoid climbers, or he might have had some other task ahead. Nachiketa wondered what motivated the climbers to reach the summit. Was it fame or glory? Was it the love of mountains? Was it the spirit of adventure? Or, perhaps, sheer call of the summit?)

Chapter 10

Understanding Organisational Change

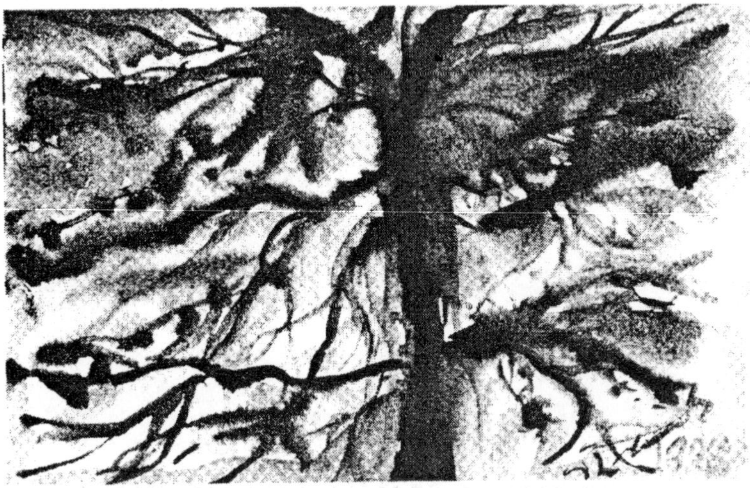

To an extent, a dialogue brings a change. In the process of our conversation, you would have observed that I started knowing better about you and you did the same about me. In fact, if I may say so in a symbolic sense, you are introjecting me and I you. You are becoming me and I you. We have a tendency to influence each other by cognitive restructuring.

7 Mantras for Managers

- ☆ *Understanding changes as the Law of Nature. So do organisations change in the flux of continuous growth and decay.*
- ☆ *Check health of organisations to arrest decay by right reality sensing and internalisation of awareness.*
- ☆ *Understand changed vision to integrate the organisation in a continuous whirlpool of changing reality.*
- ☆ *Use mission-oriented leadership to guide organisations towards their goals.*
- ☆ *Restructure organisations by changing behaviour patterns of people to positive goals.*
- ☆ *Change values and attitudes to provide glue to restructuring and develop integration.*
- ☆ *Use high pressure counselling to bring about changes in behavioural patterns.*

Yeti: After having dwelt in the realm of darkness, we need to now turn our eyes to the sunshine. Look, how a lone Sagarmatha is sparkling in the morning!

Nachiketa: Yes, darkness and light are interchanging. Change is the law of nature. The same is true of organisations. They also change.

Yeti: How do you look at this change? We are in a dialogue since long, I am Yeti and you are Nachiketa. Why don't we change? Why can't I become Nachiketa and you turn out as Yeti?

Nachiketa: That would be a complete transformation. But, to an extent, a dialogue brings a change. In the process of our conversation, you would have observed that I started knowing better about you and you did the same about me. In fact, if I may say so in a symbolic sense, you are introjecting me and I you. You are becoming me and I you. We have a tendency to influence each other by cognitive restructuring.

Yeti: But still I am Yeti and . . . . .

Nachiketa: Every entity has a core identity which gives it a differential. Perhaps, in the ultimate analysis, all reality is one; the variety is an illusion. It is how we look at things. We can simultaneously look at phenomena from an ultimate or immediate dimension. When We analyse, we define parts, give them an identity to differentiate these from each other. When we synthesise, we look at the substance and common factors. You and me belong to the same reality, in the ultimate sense. Yet we know our transitory difference of identities.

Yeti: Don't you think it is all confusing? Sometimes you are the same, sometimes you are different.

Nachiketa: Truth is bipolar. At the same time, we have night and day in different parts of the world. In each part, it is different. Yet both hemispheres are parts of one globe. Or, again, think of photons in quantum mechanics. Photons sometimes behave like waves and sometime like discrete particles. And so on.

Yeti: This is so close to seeing unity in diversity, as advocated in Upanishadic metaphysics.

Nachiketa: True, So we are changing, yet unchanging. Let us consider various changes which an organisation is prone to:

- Changes in the Mission
- Culture
- Attitudes
- Some Technological factors of future use
- Changes in building new resources
- Change in external environment through organisational pressure
- Changes in target
- Structural changes
- System changes
- Some Technological factors immediate use
- Changes in resources composition
- Change in internal environment through leadership and restructuring.

Yeti: Firstly, don't you think organisations change simply by ageing? Secondly, what is the significance of dividing them in two groups? Mission change may be done without any loss of time. Changing a simple system may take years.

Nachiketa: Organisations do tend to decay with age. But given proper reorientation and adjustment, these may grow stronger and live much longer. Unlike individuals, the life span of organisations is not determinable. Organisations like societies can continue to live long, undefinable spells depending on 'realisation' mechanisms. If organisations are insulated from internal and external reality, these trend to disintegrate. Realisation refers 'to reality-sensing and internalisation of awareness'. Realisation brings changes in the functioning of our organisations for better adjustment of their reality and long life.

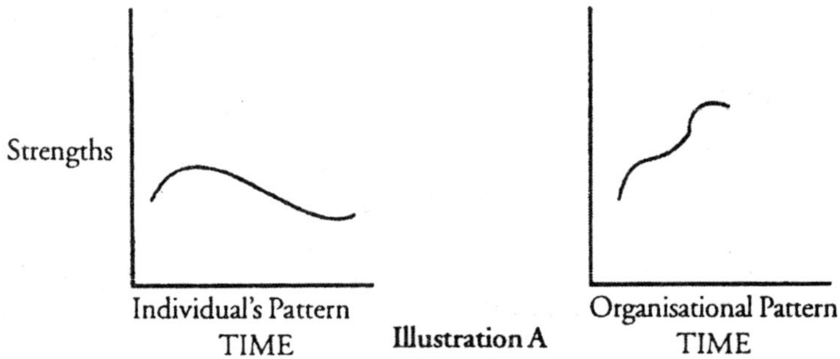

Illustration A

In other words, in order to avoid a major change, (i.e. death) continuous minor changes are essential to arrest decay.

Yeti: That means if I do not want to die, I should change continuously.

Nachiketa: To some extent, it is true for individuals also to be aware of internal, physical, psychological conditions and external climatic conditions. Proper adjustments, exercises or nourishment can help cope up with these. But the decay of human organism is determinate unlike an organisation. This is why the cycle of growth and decline of individuals and organisations varies widely.

In Illustration B, we have the so-called normal pattern. In fact, in the case of individuals, the decline or drop could be sudden in some cases, but in the case of organisations, patterns vary in every respect.

(Yeti starts laughing at figures drawn on a rock by Nachiketa. He seems to think it is a meaningless exercise. He throws a snowball at the rock obliterating all figures and laughs).

Yeti: Now where are your whirlpools?

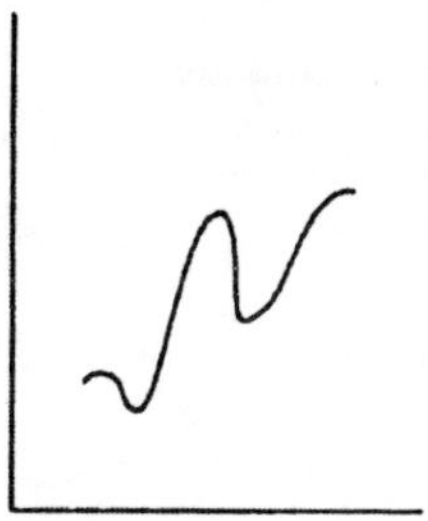

I
A Fluctuating Organisation

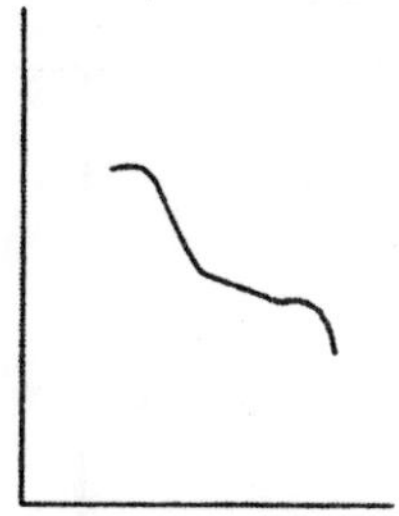

II
A Sick Organisation

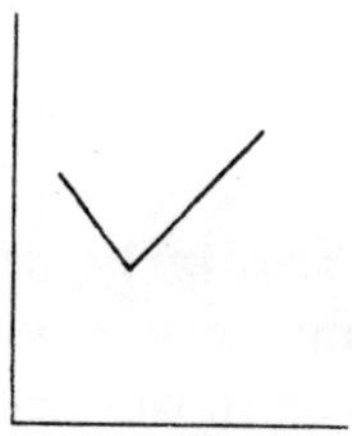

III
A Middle dip Organisation

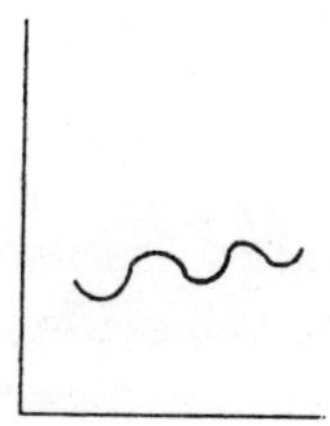

IV
A Static Organisation

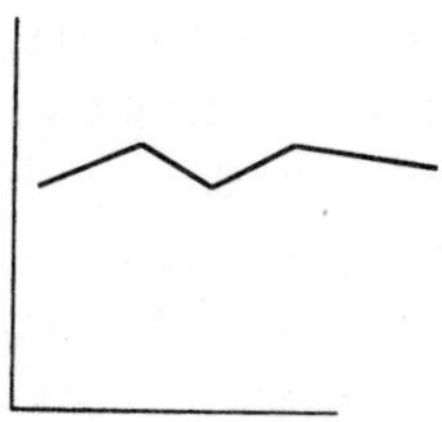

V
A Stable Organisation

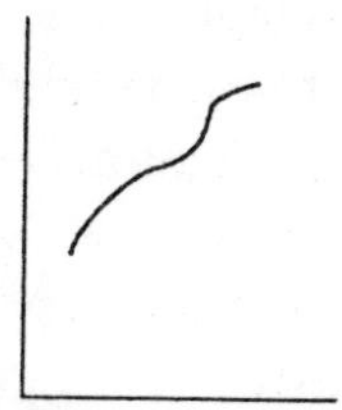

VI
A Growth-Oriented Organisation

Nachiketa: (Laughs). These are still there but not visible. (Both laugh again). Changes can be of various levels. Core changes require greater in-depth efforts. A longer period of time is required to effect core changes and are the most difficult to achieve. An individual's value system and

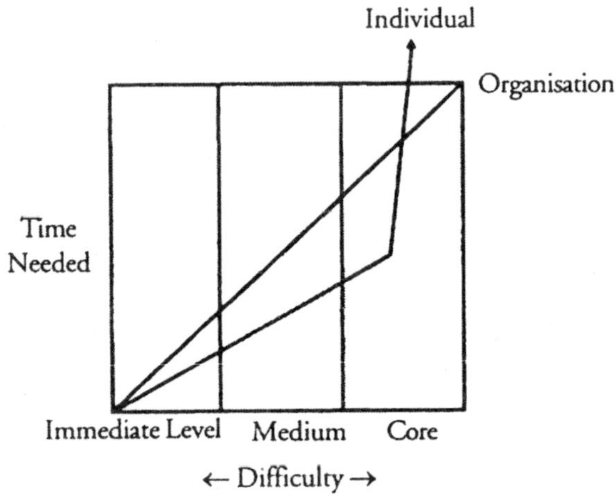

personality cannot be changed easily. Similarly an organisation's identity and values need long drawn out efforts but are more easily attainable goals than in the case of an individual. Organisations are greatly influenced by leadership as they have a great deal of power and influence on the structure and its working. A leader can change the structure overnight, which will have tremendous impact on the organisation. But in case a man decides to change his own value system or of another person, he inevitably meets the resistance from beliefs formed over decades and embedded in genetic as well as emotional realms. Restructuring an organisation is a more easily attainable goal than restructuring a personality. But even in the case of personality, it can undergo dramatic changes due to powerful traumatic experiences or metamorphosis, enlightenment, ecstasy, etc. A medium range experience is not likely to bring about changes.

Yeti: What really holds it up? Let us check on road blocks.

Nachiketa: Yes, some of the road blocks are:

- Long years of acceptance of a value as loyalty factor.
- Emotional association of a value with near and dear ones.
- Early childhood's 'imprinting' which forms deep impressions.
- Logical support to a value derived from conforming to experience and inability to recognise or fully assimilate experience which goes against the value. If we start accepting truth as good, we tend to note experiences which conform to this and do not register non-conforming experience.
- Unconscious resistance is more powerful in the case of individuals than organisations. Hence the change in human beings in more difficult to bring about than in the case of external behaviour or men needed for organisations.

Yeti: Should these organisations concentrate on behaviour change amongst its employees as against personality change?

Nachiketa: Yes and No.

Yeti: Ha! Ha! Again you are bipolar.

Nachiketa: Yes, because organisations are most concerned with some external behaviour change, which can be effected without core changes. No, because external changes could be transitory unless accompanied by deep-rooted beliefs. I think, organisations can compromise on immediate and medium level changes, which should be reinforced from time to time.

Yeti: Let us understand others.

Nachiketa: I have spoken of changes of various types as very often there is a debate on the possibility of change and we argue in a see-saw manner. In reality, we are approaching it from various levels. I only wish to say change is possible and can be brought about in values and attitudes-but in a short-term only at immediate level.

Yeti: How does one know what is immediate level?

- Whether the change can be done without changing personality.
- Whether it can be effected without total restructuring.
- Whether it is possible without bringing about wider changes in society.
- Whether it is within the ambit of day-to-day functioning of organisations.

Take, for example, attendance and overtime. These are not very deep-rooted changes. But if one wants to change peoples basic values of loyalty or patriotism, it is just not possible in the near future or without a major catastrophe. I have developed recently a method to change attitudes of some women employees to attendance. Earlier they took it casually. They did not pay much heed to the value of regular attendance. We introduced a method which we now call 'High Pressure Interviews', and we found it brought about a lot of changes.

Yeti: What is this new game 'HPI' or Hippy?

Nachiketa: It consists of:

- Creating tension amongst the employees.
- Detailed questioning and exploration of reasons.
- Firm advice to change the attitudes.

- Making it clear that you care for people but if they do not perform their roles well, they will reap the consequences.
- Vigorous personal follow-up.

Yeti: Why create tensions?

Nachiketa: When you want to bend a piece of iron, you have to heat it up. Any human being who does not see the necessity of change has to be 'prepared' for this change. He should understand the importance of changing. In the case quoted by me, the girls were given charge-sheets, memos, warnings, etc., but they were indifferent. They were put through tensed situations like making them wait for hours for the interview, refusal to put them on duly for quite some time and then finally interviewing them. The results are as under:

Absenteeism before HPI Average absence per Month	Absenteeism after one month of HPI Average absence per month	Absenteeism after six months Average absence per month
17.4%	9.9%	2.5%

Yeti: That is a dramatic change!

Nachiketa: Yes, that is how people can change but this process has to continue and be followed up.

Yeti was humming a song. Perhaps tension was growing on him. He threw his bottle in the valley down below and growled. Quietly he disappeared behind the mountain. Was he resisting a change? Or, was he changing?

Chapter 11

Perception of Reality and Creativity

The theme of the present dialogue revolves round perception of reality, how organisational effectiveness is related to accurate perception, and how men can enhance their power of 'word watching'. In essence, creativity symbolises the peak of human endeavour. The development and growth of civilisation will depend on creative faculties of the human race. Destruction is inevitable but the process of giving life to ideas is singularly man's distinction. Finally the end is the same.

7 Mantras for Managers

- *Empower organisation by accurate perception of reality and right decision-making.*
- *Create new psycho-maps of organisation by imagination and dreams.*
- *Cultivate creativity as a means to understanding organisations and changing them.*
- *Use seven steps to right reality sensing through tranquillity, creativity, clarity, detachment, multiple checking objectivity and a perception of totality.*
- *Build creativity by seven steps of exploration, thinking, searching, debating, evaluating, picture building and discovery.*
- *Challenge convention, rituals and age-old accepted assumptions.*
- *Think free for multiplying options and choices in finding new ways.*

Nachiketa: All along we talked of organisational themes. We developed some artifacts. Perhaps some toys to play. Let us see if understanding organisations really adds to our ability for improving these.

Yeti: Understanding is feeling, not rationalising. You seem to get lost in verbiage. What do you have finally? Words, words and words!

Nachiketa: Yes, some words! But words denote feelings, ideas and thoughts. These are symbols just as touch is. Feelings can be perceived through:

- touch
- seeing
- sound or hearing
- interpreting signs
- words/figures/statistics
- facial expressions
- eyes
- various parts of body and their movements, e.g., hands, feet, postures, etc.

The external aspects of organisation:

- Machines
- Tables/chairs/buildings
- Groups of people
- Inner feeling (sixth sense, hunch, gut feeling).

Yeti: But all this is again too intricate.

Nachiketa: Could be unless we know what all this means.

Yeti: But why should we know?

Nachiketa: That is precisely the point. Any organisation, which has accurate perception of its internal and external reality, has adequate capability of taking right decisions to enhance its effectiveness. Conversely, ineffective organisations tend to falter on reality sensing and hence are not capable of creative responses. Let me explain to you some typical perceptional models (See Illustration A).

Yeti: Do you mean it is so simple that if you see properly, you can do better?

Nachiketa: In a sense, yes. The process of decision making by leadership of an organisation is closely dependent on the individual and collective perception of reality by its leaders. The process of reality sensing is paramount in determining the decision making. A wrong reality sense is bound to dictate wrong decisions.

Illustration A

Types	Perceptional Fault	Key elements	Symptoms
Internally weak organisation	Organisations which fail to sense the internal environment	Employees, groups, talented managers, internal strengths & weakness, strategic planning.	Poor IR, lack of motivation, groupism, too much rumour mongering, high costs, uncontrolled expenses, poor tools/equipment.
Externally weak organisation	Organisations which fail to sense the external event.	Public and press developments, markets, technology and strategies for future	Bad public image, criticism, technology obsolescence, reduced competitiveness.
Sick organisations	Organisations which fail to sense both external and internal environments.	All the above	Closure, deaths.

Yeti: So, what you mean is that once I perceive the summit and difficulties on the way rightly, the climbing is sure.

Nachiketa: No, not necessarily. What route you choose depends on the choice of your mind. A creative mind is capable of choosing creative solutions. Even if the reality sensing is correct, a non-creative mind may make a wrong choice. It is just like a number of programmes available on a computer. It is a mental decision to choose one. Even developing a variety of programmes is a mental act.

Yeti: So. Why do all this? Why not develop a creative mind? Everything seems to be creation of our mind. You are going back to *Vedanta*.

Nachiketa: You are very right. Organisations are creations of mind. That is why they need more imagination. Organisations are not products of nature but mental frameworks. That is why the mission and objectives are the psycho-maps, which we draw up to scale the summit. We shall separately deal with creativity of mind but, for the time being, let us be clear that the raw data for development and choice of alternatives comes from right reality sensing. If the data is not correct, all our programmes will go haywire.

Yeti: But how do we develop right data?

Nachiketa: By accurate perception which is possible through a fourfold process.

Mind ⇔ Interpretation ⇒ Senses ⇔ External reality / Internal reality

Mind interpretation senses external reality and internal reality. Mind is not a passive receiver but active in interpretation. When a boy returns from school, a mother hears footsteps and thinks her son has come. She has not seen the son. She is interpreting the sound of footsteps at a particular time and her daily experience. In life, we interpret thousands of events like this. The process of interpretation, therefore, is as important as hearing rightly. If a mother is too anxious or worried about the child, she hears every footstep sound as the return of her son. In this case, interpretations is distorted by a disturbed mind. Tranquillity and equilibrium are, therefore, essential prerequisites of a clear mind to understand the organisational reality. Detachment or non-possessiveness is absolutely essential for right feeling and seeing.

Yeti: Like Buddha, you can say: Seven steps to right reality sensing are:

- Develop a tranquil mind.
- Interpret creatively: Develop various possibilities and choose one.
- Hear dispassionately.
- See clearly.
- Feel dispossessively.
- Cross-check by using more than one senses or sources.
- Perceive the totality.

Nachiketa: It is a clever summary. But all this depends on the quality and creativity of mind. We have been talking of quality of life and work and not the quality of mind.

Yeti: What can you do with that? It is what you have.

Nachiketa: To a great extent. But, to some extent, one can develop it. Let us, however, first discuss on what to choose to perceive reality. You know sound has pre-eminence in *Vedas*, these were transmitted through sound waves and not the written word for ages. Today seeing is more important as computer flashes readings on the screen or pages of data are thrown your table. A manager today uses his eyes more than other senses. It is a pity that sometime presentations are made in all darkness through films, videos and slides. The contact between man and man is lost. You merely watch papers or screens. This tends to reduce the feeling of direct contact.

Yeti: But you are in contact with screens. I am in contact with mountains and not men. It does not mean my understanding of reality is poor.

Nachiketa: Reality is neither on paper nor on screen. It is an inside or outside life. Organisms and nature lend us a sense of living a life. Looking at mountains or oceans can be as precious an insight on cosmic feeling as during the pages of an epic or stored insights on a screen. Both are fascinating. But too much of artificial sensations reduce the natural feel of life. It is absolutely essential to sense the reality, to go to places on the field, at various locations, talk to people, look in their eyes, take a stride to sense their existence, and to groups in action. The most needed skill of 'world watching' is less popular than 'bird watching'. We must teach leaders and managers the art of observation and feeling for man and nature. 'World watching' is a dispassionate, not indifferent, but warm reaching-out to your linkages in the environment to perceive the totality in its naked glory, shorn of secondary sources like paper or cassettes drapery.

Yeti: Now you are getting poetic.

Nachiketa: I agree I saw Pine trees and Deodars on my way to Shimla. It was a sight, which touched the innermost strings of my heart. Imagine how Wordworth would have gone ecstatic at the sight of daffodils. I saw great fantasy and dreams in the needles of pines. I admired the strength and majesty of Deodars. Trees are very beautiful reminders of nature's classic value. These are blurred by the dust of metropolitan transport or industrial ashes. That is why we need more trees. In Tokyo, you see male and female trees side by side. I forget the names of these Japanese trees but these are very pretty. Again they provide a relief from the brick and mortar civilisation of today.

Yeti: I find you more I love with trees but you never noticed tall Deodars around us in Himalayas.

Nachiketa: I confess that trees are wonderful but sometimes we get so much engaged in our concepts, mundane life or rough and tumble of life that we do not admire these. Do you remember that after the famous clothes-stealing episode, when Krishna was returning, he stopped in the forest on the way just gazing at the trees for a long time. The cowherd boys could not understand what he was doing for so long. "What are you doing now?", they asked. How much sun and rain these trees bear on themselves, and how much shade or comfort these give to others, Krishna answered. I think this is the greatest tribute to trees. It is a message of sensitivity and creativity. This really is projection of a great mind on the natural objects. Also it shows how keen was the power of observation of Krishna.

Yeti: Now you are confusing trees with reality.

Nachiketa: No, I am just interpreting signs and symbols of reality. One can just look at a tree and say it is a tree. It is interpretation with a mind which makes the difference. Hence the question of right perception. Any insignificant thing can stand out in its meanings, once we are keen on observing it and seeing it as a symbol. After all, as we have seen, all cues are subject to mental interpretation.

Yeti: This leads us to creativity.

Nachiketa: True. A creative mind can interpret the cues in much better, varied and new terms. A creative mind finds a link, where none seems to exist to an ordinary mind. There lies the value of creativity. In organisational growth, it plays a significant role. The future will place greater demand on creativity of leaders and organisational men, since the options will become greater demand on creativity of leaders and organisational men, since the options will become enormously large or the problems will become amenable to new solutions.

Yeti: If the options are too many, what is the use of creativity?

Nachiketa: Creativity will help in synthesising these for 'best fit' or optimum results.

Yeti: Let us continue with your creativity syndrome.

Nachiketa: It is not a syndrome. It is the essence of development and living.

Yeti: You mean to say people like me are dead!

Nachiketa: No. You too are a very ingenious and creative person. But even if one is not, he does not cease to exist. Existence is not living. Living is conscious; an awareness phenomenon. It is not an amoeba's monotonous motions.

Yeti: But everyone who thinks has a mind. Every human being is living.

Nachiketa: Everyone who thinks has a mind, but everyone who has a mind does not think. I wish everyone who thinks, really thinks. Thinking is a process of insight and discovery.

Yeti: But even deception of thinking is thinking.

Nachiketa: True, but it is only a deception. An exploration of alternative modes of behaviour and patterns leads to creativity. Let me not repeat what is repetitiously being written by behavioural scientists. I shall take you to thinking or understanding of creativity from my point of view. When a chimpanzee is finding new ways (new for him) to get hold of a fruit, he is thinking. When he is expecting food, he is needing. When he is searching food, he is exploring, when he is finding ways to search food thinking. Search is not enough for thinking. Need can spark the process. What is needed is the ways of developing alternatives, finding new connections, new techniques and new options.

Yeti: So there lies your creation—the prized product of thinking.

Nachiketa: No, the prized process and product.

Yeti: But how does it relate to organisations?

Nachiketa: In many ways:

FIRST

When a manager chooses a view of reality, it depends on what are his creative abilities to build a variety of scenarios and develop their possibilities on an objective basis.

SECOND

After various scenarios are developed, the most important issue is how he responds to these. Not only which he chooses but also which response he chooses out of various alternatives created by him.

THIRD

After he responds to the options, how best he evaluates and which one he selects finally? All these are important stages of creative process.

The point I am trying to make is that a less creative man has 'black and white' vision. The 'colour' vision needs versatility of available paints and brushes to depict the reality. A creative man finds his own way of looking at things and developing best fit responses. He, therefore, contributes to growth and development by finding options and multiple routes. His summit is richer, better and more his own.

Yeti: What are elementary processes apart from a monkey's ways?

(Yeti giggles)

Nachiketa: If we look at the same elementary process in human beings, we find distinct stages. These stages are not necessarily separate or rigidly in chronological order. These may overlap or change order in various persons or at different times.

- *Receiving cues*: This is a stage when signs and symbols are stored. Data is collected and information is gained.
- *Churning state*: It involves brooding over the problem or vision along with information.
- *Searching way*: It involves multiplying option, ideas, concepts. It is running through the maze in different routes.
- *Talking self*. One starts debating with oneself about what options are possible and their pros and cons.
- *Evaluation*: This is sifting the chaff from the grain.
- *Picture building*: Mentally one imagines the concept and sees it through in its functioning or taking shape. It is imagining the idea, out there as a living thing or product. By this process one may re-build the picture, if needed.

Insight: Final stage when idea/solutions are clear. These shine like bright sunny tops of mountains. These are distant but clear.

Yeti: I think we seem to be reaching a stage when our insights are becoming clear but our minds are becoming marshes. Sometimes I feel it is better to be dumb and dull than searching for all the creative options. Is life not too complicated the way you wish to make it! Are we slaves of a creative Frankenstein or are we free to live the way we find natural? Are we able to capture either life or death by any process? Even if we do that, is it worth being conditioned to a test tube or computerised cardiac system?

Nachiketa: I know we have reached where we really started the process. In the process we learnt a lot but I agree that beginnings and ends are the same.

(Yeti threw of the bottle of whisky down the mountain cliff. He laughed and laughed. He ran to the highest cliff, stood there as if ready to fly down the creek. He appeared in silhouette like Icarus. The sun seemed to be slipping down behind the hills. Nachiketa could see his shadow on the rocks. Suddenly he shouted something in joy and jumped down as if trying to fly. Nachiketa could see him rolling down over snows thousands of feet down till he disappeared. Nachiketa was puzzled. Did Yeti make a tryst with creative death? Did he really know how to fly and is still alive or was it an illusion? Yeti seemed a mystery. Yeti did not come. Nachiketa looked at the mountains and trees. He had no one to communicate, to argue and laugh with. White Sagarmatha was as mute as ever; it was the only witness to all the games. A few days later, some explorers said they heard strange sounds of 'Beginnings are ends and ends are beginnings'. They did not know how these words echoed in the valley. Was Yeti moving in spirit! Nachiketa again shouted in the valley for Yeti 'Where are you? The echoes came back sharp, "Where are you? Where are you?" again and again.)

Postscript to the Fourth Edition

Yeti is today as much a buzzword for managers and students as it has been to Everest climbers centuries back. This edition 'Mantras for Managers' is new incarnation of Yeti's dialogues? During one of my visits to Europe, I was amazed to see in the office of a Head of Business School an inscription which read:

Question: Have you really seen Yeti?

Answer: Have you really seen yourself?

—*The Dialogues with Yeti*

After a decade of existence, it has earned a place for itself in global management thought. Strangely, its intuition remains as valid today as it was at the time of its first publication. On the other hand, it is proving prophetic on all its essential ideas. Some examples are given below after a comparative study of current literature and futurologists' peep into 2000.

Significant ideas in this book in 1980s	Ideas for 2000 as stated in research result in 1990s
• Organisations are living being but 'cycle of growth' and decline of individuals and organisations varies widely.	Organisations are living beings and no longer considered machines.

• Future will place great demand on creativity of leaders.	Freedom and individual creativity will be the single most important driving force behind next millennium (Greald Celente in Trends 2000).
• Cultural impact on management is tremendous.	Culture/attitudes will determine performance of economics.
• Perception and intution are key to effective management.	Many of the Western management thinkers propound similar views. Mintzberg argues: "Intuition is the soft belly of management.
• Learning is core of human and organisational development.	Peter Senge Propelled the term 'the Learning organisation' to the forefront of the corporates (1990). Knowledge for Development, report the World Bank for 1999 indicates that poor countries differ from rich not only because they have less capital but because they have less knowledge.
• Ideologies of communism and capitalism should yield to humanism inter-relatedness becoming.	Both have suffered in USSR and far East Asia. Interdependence is more clear.
• Profit and money are not the most important aims of organisation.	Many countries of Europe and Japan rate profit as not highest aim. (Trompennar).
• Truth of feeling counts in the ultimate analysis.	A shift to feeling from pure logic is being recognised. E.g. fuzzy logic.
• Nature is a great teacher and we should go back to it from time to time.	Nations will return to nature and great outdoors—a trend to catch fire in 2000s (Trends 2000).

Yeti would say, "Profound thoughts are forever". The Fourth Reprint of this book, therefore, is a tribute to the eternal spirit of Yeti-free, natural, primordial and loving. Dr Sigmund Freud once said: "Happiness is a deferred fulfilment of a primordial wish. That is why, money gives so little, as money cannot be an infantile wish." Yeti with his innocent intuition and natural charm exhorts you to 'think and feel together with cycle of change in Nature: As winter gives way to spring, the cycle of nature remains inexorable. We all are part of this cosmic process of eternal flux. A great Urdu poet summarised this up:

Hum Muvahid hain, hamara kaish hai tarke-e-rasoom
Millaten jab mit gayen, adjza-e-iman hogayeen

—*Ghalib*

I believe in one cosmic force, my style outthrows conventions when small distinctions disappear, they merge in great faith.

Let not technology and science delude us to feel that we can subjugate the phenomena of nature. We have to live in harmony with it. Managers and leaders have also to imbibe the writing on the wall in their life and work. Hellinistic view of conquest is fast yielding place to Oriental view that man organisation co-exist as a part of universal architecture.

N K SINGH
Delhi School of Business
April, 1999

Postscript to the Third Edition

This third edition of 'the Dialogues' is a steady reminder of its demand. I was happy to note that my students and some of their parents seemed to enjoy the Dialogues a lot. A student has founded a company with its name. Many corporate managers have carried it as a creative companion to read it from time to time for new insights. Even when I re-read it, I feel as if it is written by some wild sage, whom I knew well. Yeti is now a corporate talisman.

It is also a great satisfaction that now many western gurus are treading the same path. It is more and more clear that ultimate values cannot be obliterated in the chaotic market rat-race. The more one distances oneself from these profound truths and nature, the more one suffers from soul troubles. Even medical men are turning to Yeti - Nachiketa synthesis of treating health and life holistically. I am only compelled to repeat; 'Profound thoughts are forever'. On a separate plane, I wrote poetry in the same vein for a companion volume 'Yeti's Haikus'. Let us also read poetry in management classes and offices to refresh our minds lest they become sick of cut-throat pollution and corporate anorexia.

N K SINGH

Postscript to the Second Revised Edition

I had an option to revise this book when it was going for the second edition but I was taken in by an innocent remark of Ms. Veronika Klemencic of Ljubljana, who thought it is a sacred book. And sacred books are not revised! Although it is profane and irreverent yet it rings true. Some friends asked me to add case studies which I thought would change its allegorical character. Others wanted me to drop Swami Ranganathananda's comments. I refused to do so. The reason is simple. What Swamiji is saying is perfectly in tune with his perception and role but what I see and experience is my way. Truth is not the monopoly of those who profess they only know. In *Tantra,* one passes through the sensual delights to spiritual sphere. There are many roads to a destination. I have been teaching my students that I am a spiritualist and not a religious man. While spiritualism is a matter of experience, religion is a matter of faith. Yeti might say, "you drink spirits and that makes you spiritualist." I do not wish to dispute his vision.

In the end, readers might say what do the dialogues teach? I would only say it is a cafeteria where you might have "your" choice. I have presented the kaleidoscope of man and organisations. I find ultimately an experience of truth, beauty and noble feelings determine the quality of mind.

Even effective organisations depend on people who have nourished these values in their thoughts and actions. This little book is a stimulant for creative thinking. No wonder even contemporary experts such as Tom Peter talk Yeti-like while serving self-destruct menu with icing of intellect and imagination as ultimate resources of organisations. Going forward today also means simultaneously going backward. I want to synthesise Eastern and Western ways of thoughts to develop the future approach to management. Management has been drowned in Western marshes for too long. It is time to recover it and place it in a holistic perspective.

Finally management transcends sectoral concerns to become global. Globalisation is the current buzzword but a time will come when cosmocisation could be the burning craze. Man will find peace in struggle, interdependence in competitive edge, and creative enhancement in downsizing. The organisations of future-stars or constellations will pattern their intricate designs on natures' forms and networks. Creative renewal only will re-engineer man and organisations close to nature. The most sophisticated tool of management is the mind of the man, which is central to all change and development. More we know about it less we understand it. Intuition, perception and creativity are the windows to its depths. Let us peep into the valley of mind with child like curiosity and wonder.

N K SINGH
Adhitam Kendra
Fore School of Management
January, 1995
New Delhi